Sandra M. Schneiders

D0729763

Beyond Patching

Faith and Feminism
in the Catholic Church

REVISED EDITION

Paulist Press ◆ **New York** ◆ **Mahwah, N.J.**

To Paul and Greg
Brothers, friends, and dialogue partners
With love

THE ANTHONY JORDAN LECTURES
1990
NEWMAN THEOLOGICAL COLLEGE
EDMONTON

Copyright © 1991, 2004 by Sandra M. Schneiders, IHM

Library of Congress Cataloging-in-Publication Data

Schneiders, Sandra M.
    Beyond patching : faith and feminism in the Catholic Church / by Sandra
M. Schneiders.
        p.cm.
    Originally presented as the 1990 Anthony Jordan lectures in theology
given at Newman Theological College in Edmonton, Alta.
    Includes bibliographical references.
    ISBN 0-8091-4282-1
    1. Feminism—Religious aspects—Catholic Church. 2. Catholic Church—
Doctrines. I. Title. II. Title: Anthony Jordan annual lectures in theology.
    BX2347.8W6S25   1991
    261.8'3442—dc20   90-46866
                                                                                   CIP

Published by Paulist Press
997 Macarthur Boulevard
Mahwah, New Jersey 07430

www.paulistpress.com

Printed and bound in the United States of America

Contents

"No one sews a piece of unshrunk cloth
on an old garment; for the patch would pull away
from it, the new from the old, and a worse
tear would be made." Mark 2:21

Preface to the Second Edition

When I delivered the Anthony Jordan Lectures on Faith and Feminism in the Catholic Church, which were published as *Beyond Patching* in 1990, I could not have guessed that the crisis of male domination and oppression in the Church that I described in relation to women would, some ten years later, be rendered so shockingly graphic in the scandal of clerical sexual abuse of children that began to emerge into public view in 2000. Many people do not yet see the intimate connection between the sexually-based oppression of women by powerful males and the sexual domination and exploitation of children by powerful males. Feminists, however, do see the connection. Patriarchy is the system of domination which legitimates the oppression of the weak by the powerful, and it is rooted in the primordial and prototypical hierarchical dualism of male over female. Children share women's vulnerability to the powerful, and in both cases male-controlled religion is used to legitimate abuse of the vulnerable. People who subscribe to the ideology of patriarchy, especially its sacralized form as hierarchy, regard what men, especially men with sacralized identities and roles, do to women and children as their right. Today that "right" is being called into question in the public forum as perhaps never before in history, at least in the history of the Church.[1] Consequently, this seems a good time to offer a second edition of this "primer" on feminism that challenges patriarchy in principle and in practice, discusses the role of scripture as both part of the problem and a potential resource for a liberationist approach, and points out the critical gravity of our responsibility to address gender- and sex-based injustice and violence in our Church.

Although much has changed since 1990, much has also remained the same. I want to emphasize what has changed, because therein lie new resources for hope. But let me begin by noting briefly some things that have not changed significantly since 1990. First, the existence, nature, and basic commitments of feminism, both as a cultural movement in society and as an ecclesial and spiritual phenomenon in the Church (the subject matter of chapter 1), are very much alive and well. Second, the efforts within the religious and secular academies, especially in biblical studies and theology (the subject of chapter 2), have continued, deepened, and internally diversified in important ways as scholars have recognized the distinctive experiences of women of different races, classes, educational opportunities, and geographic locations. And third, the struggle of feminist Catholic women and their male allies for women's full inclusion in the life of the Church (the subject of chapter 3) not only continues but has broadened and deepened as increasing numbers of Catholics become aware of both the injustice of women's ecclesiastical marginalization and exclusion and the critical need of the whole Church for women's ministerial gifts.

Sadly, what also has not changed is the adamant resistance of ecclesiastical leadership to the work of the Holy Spirit calling women into full Christian personhood and

participation in the life of the Church. Despite the effu-
sively romantic "feminist" rhetoric of some official documents attempting to elevate a fatally flawed "dual
anthropology" to the level of Church teaching, the commitment of the Vatican to male supremacy and female
subordination in the Church remains firmly in place.[2] Its
demise seems ever more inevitable, but as yet this is a
hope rather than a reality.

More important, however, than official intransigence
is the really significant changes that have occurred in the
past decade that are affecting the feminist discourse within
the Church. Although it would be impossible, because of
both restrictions of space and the limitations of my competence, to catalogue, much less adequately explore, the
full range of pertinent changes, I will highlight some rep-
resentative developments in western culture, the academy, and the Church that seem particularly relevant to
our topic.

Perhaps the most pervasive, and also most difficult
to define or describe, *cultural development* of the past
quarter-century is the emergence of what cultural critics
are calling *postmodernity*.[3] This development is more like
a change in the atmosphere or the air we breathe than the
arrival of an explicit doctrine or even an ideology.
Postmodernism is, as the label suggests, an ethos that is
succeeding and gradually undermining what we have
called "modernity." Both modernity and its successor are
characterized by many positive and negative features
that we hardly notice in our day-to-day lives even though
they influence our thoughts, emotions, relationships, and
behaviors in profound and pervasive ways.

Modernity, the successor to the Middle Ages, places
its ultimate confidence in science (rather than in faith, as
did our medieval forebears), which it regards as the uni-

versally valid, unarguable basis of whatever "absolute" truth is available to humans.[4] Even in the area of theology, which is an essentially faith-based discourse, that which seems incompatible with contemporary science is regarded as untenable.[5] And humanity is at the center and the apex of the reality that science explains. Everything revolves around us, and all things exist for our use and enjoyment. Our individual human rights, the only rights that exist, are sacred and inalienable and to be defended at all costs. Progress, defined as what meets the needs and wants of humans, especially those with abundant material resources, is always desirable. And there is an uncritical, if not cynical, confidence that if everyone looks after their own needs and wants, eventually everyone will flourish.

Even noting these few working assumptions of modernity highlights its scientism, anthropocentrism, reductionistic naturalism, progressivism, and individualism. Although modernity has generated much genuine human good—such as life-enhancing medical advances, scientific development, democracy, the struggle for human rights and dignity, as well as the struggle for the physical and mental well-being of humans everywhere—it has also generated a rapacious capitalism driven by artificially generated "needs" and unbridled greed, economic globalization that victimizes the poor for the benefit of the rich, devastating ecological degradation, and much else that urgently demands rectification if the species and the cosmos are to survive.[6]

Postmodernism shares the moral ambiguity of the modernism to which it is a challenge and an alternative. In other words, as with modernism, there is much about postmodernism that offers resources for a better world and much that is problematic. Postmodernism's relativizing of false absolutes in every sphere has great potential for opening minds to new visions of truth. Its attention to diversity and to the marginal is turning our attention to the "other" in our midst and encouraging movements on every continent toward liberation of the oppressed. But there is also much about postmodernism that is potentially destructive, especially its tendency toward total and nihilistic relativism, its potentially fatal fascination with meaninglessness, and the subsequent abdication of personal and corporate responsibility.

The importance of the emergence of postmodernism for feminism lies in its relativization of hegemonic systems, whether religious, cultural, artistic, economic, political, social, or other.[7] The postmodern sensibility is spontaneously suspicious of and critical toward any ideology, system, or arrangement that claims to be the "whole take" on anything. It is a mentality that wants to listen without a priori judgments to all opinions, try out many solutions, experience widely if not indiscriminately, put things together that have been kept separate, abolish boundaries, and privilege the unusual, the unexpected, the fragmentary, or the heretofore unnoticed or unheard. It challenges any metanarrative, that is, any "master story" that claims to account for all reality according to some unitary scheme in which everything has a pre-assigned place and "makes sense," because "sense" has been established before all the data has been examined or even before some of it existed. From the adolescent who combs her hair into purple spikes or pierces his nose or dresses like Batman on an ordinary school day, to the millionaire dotcom executive who walks to the office shirtless in dirty socks, to the householder who combines several aesthetically clashing styles in the same room, to the literary critic who interprets a text into a pile of verbal rubble for the sheer pleasure of subverting accepted notions of meaning, to the new-ager who pieces together a private religion of "spare parts"—people influenced by the ethos of postmodernism resist the pre-established, the unquestioned, the dominant, the "one right answer," the "truth" that "everyone knows." Subversion, de-stabilization, relativization, novelty, and resistance are the focus of postmodern concern.

But the postmodern sensibility has more constructive expressions than purple hair and more serious agendas than literary nihilism. The tendency to question differently, to privilege the silenced and ignored, to look at reality from "below" or from "outside," to include what has been excluded, to dethrone what has had unquestioned power is a fundamental contribution of postmodernism to the liberationist agenda that has empowered the emergence of colonized peoples and the uprising of the poor.

Feminism is, in many ways, a postmodern enterprise. The patriarchal master story in which maleness was considered normative of humanity and powerful males determined who and what was important in world history (and indeed what constituted "world" and what counted as "history") is the story in which women existed as support systems for men, in which women and children were considered male property for male use and pleasure,and in which femaleness itself was defined as a defective form of humanity and thus an impediment to full participation in society or Church. Subverting that patriarchal master story and its implications is basic to the agenda of feminism. Twenty-five years ago this agenda looked like the revolt of some (mostly privileged, white) women malcontents who wanted a piece of the male pie. Today, in the context of an increasingly postmodern men-

tality, it is more likely to be seen as a liberationist movement that shares with other such movements a commitment to the empowerment of the oppressed "other."
Many in our culture no longer see the patriarchal master
story as the self-evident "way things are" or, even worse,
the "divine plan of how things should be," but as the
falsely universalized, self-serving reality-construction of
those who benefit from it to the detriment of those it
oppresses.

This relativization of the patriarchal ideology and
agenda has "mainstreamed" feminist criticism. It no longer
appears as a "women's issue" but as a human issue intimately linked to the struggle of people of color, children,
the mentally and physically disabled, the laity, immigrants,
the poor, and all those in society who are, for some reason, "other" to the hegemonic group of white, western,
affluent males.

Another major contribution of the postmodern sensibility to the feminist agenda is its positive evaluation of
the "other" precisely *as* other, that is, not merely as the
oppressed in need of liberation but as a contributor of
what is not available from one's own kind. Modernity's
response to the other was often the attempt to neutralize,
if not obliterate, its otherness or difference. This could be
done by putting "them" (the mentally ill, the racially different) away in institutions or "homelands," or by annihi-
lating them (as in the Nazi "final solution" to Jewish
otherness), or by marginalizing, suppressing, or ignoring
them (as with women and children), or even by "con-
verting" those who thought or believed differently, even
if done by indoctrination. The quintessential "other" in
every society and class and throughout history has been
"woman." The very fact that the term "woman" has usually been used in the singular when discussing the

"woman problem" bears witness to the generic, stereo-typed approach to half the human race as simply "the other." Gradually feminism has taught the teachable that there is no such thing as "woman," only women who are individuals as different from one another in many respects as they are alike, and as much like some men as they are different from others.

Increasingly, contemporary people are seeing that "otherness" can mean not merely difference but enrich-ment. The other may bring not a deviant (and therefore, by definition, inferior) experience, position, or idea but some-thing unique to which one would not otherwise have access. Although this is still far from the universal (or even majority) position, there is increasing evidence that busi-ness, politics, the professions, the arts, and ordinary daily life are enriched by the diversity of experience of those who participate and consequently by an increasing com-mitment to inclusivity. There is a real difference between a legal profession in which people of color are on, and not only in front of, the bench and one in which all judges and lawyers are white males and most defendants are people of color. A business in which women hold top executive posi-tions is not compromised but has new resources available for growth and development. And a soccer team on which boys and girls, Asian and American children play together really does create a "whole new ballgame."

The valuing of diversity in experience, sensibility, cultural conditioning, and relationality is leading many people in society and in the Church to question and even abandon the assumption that good leadership means male leadership and that women are "naturally called" to sub-servience. They want to experience the richness women can bring not only to business, the academy, and politics but to ministry and leadership in the Church. And as people open themselves to the gifts of women, they increasingly experience themselves not as the condescending "promoters" of unfortunate inferiors but as the beneficiaries of a whole new range of skills and contributions.

In the *academy*, both the religious academy of seminaries and schools of theology and the secular academy, there have also been major changes over the last two decades that bode well for the eventual success of the feminist agenda in the Church.[8] From being a fringe concern, even a case of "special pleading" for preferential treatment by incompetent women who could not meet the demands of the academy, feminism has become a respected *mainstream feature of all serious academic work*. No one teaching theology today can pretend that the work of feminist biblical scholars, systematic and moral theologians, pastoral theorists and practitioners, Church historians, or liturgists can be ignored without prejudice to the very integrity of one's work.[9] In good schools of theology no student today will graduate without having read some of these scholars and grasped both the competence they share with their male counterparts and the distinctiveness of their contributions. Indeed, in the better schools they will have had the opportunity to study with Catholic and Protestant feminist scholars, both women and men.

Feminism, in tandem with other liberationist approaches in the academy, has fully established the fact that there is no such thing as presuppositionless interpretation or non-located theologizing. If the theology of a white scholar is different from that of a Hispanic or an Asian scholar, the theology of a man is different from that of a woman. Competent scholars no longer think that male theology is simply "theology" and that the theology done by a woman is "women's theology." All theology, whether done by a woman or a man, by an American or an African, is "local theology," that is, it is regional reflection striving toward the universal by its very acknowledgement and criticism of its own regionality.

This increasing sensitivity to presuppositions and location among scholars has led to increasing differentiation within feminism itself. We are much more conscious today that there is no such thing as "feminism" but only "feminisms." White scholars cannot speak for women of color, nor first-world scholars for two-thirds-world women. The affluent cannot speak for the poor. The privileged must certainly strive to increase the opportunities of those with fewer resources and limited access, but this has to be an attempt to listen and learn and not a presumption to represent the other.[10]

As more and more women enter the conversation bringing an ever-greater diversity of women's experience to expression, the feminist agenda in the Church is maturing. From a fairly narrow focus on women's ordination, the agenda has broadened and deepened. Nothing short of the full recognition of the full humanity of all women, in family, society, and Church can respond to the feminist vision. And women's full humanity cannot be affirmed and honored unless all those who are oppressed—not only because of gender but also because of color, class, sexual orientation, ethnicity, age, or any other qualification—are likewise fully recognized, affirmed, and honored. The feminist vision is one of universal shalom in God's reign of justice, peace, and truth.

Finally, there have been several significant developments in the Church over the past two decades that have positively affected the feminist agenda. I will highlight two of these developments. Perhaps the most important, whose emergence I noted in the first edition of *Beyond Patching,* came to resounding public expression in the *Madeleva Manifesto,* formulated and proclaimed at the millennial Madeleva Convergence at St. Mary's College, Notre Dame, on April 29, 2000.[11] It consists in the explicit recognition by feminist Catholics that what they are talking about and promoting is not a baptized version of secular feminism but "evangelical" or *"Gospel feminism."* In other words, women who have remained faithful participants in the Church while becoming ever more committed feminists have come to an explicit awareness that they are not simply trying to achieve in the Church and for Catholics what feminists in general are trying to achieve for women in society. They are claiming as their own the agenda of Jesus in the Gospel, what he called "the coming of the reign of God," and insisting that feminist commitment is not just compatible with but is integral to commitment to the Gospel. The 1971 Synod of Bishops declared, "Action on behalf of justice and participation in the transformation of the world fully appear to us as a constitutive dimension of the preaching of the Gospel, or, in other words, of the Church's mission for the redemption of the human race and its liberation from every oppressive situation."[12] If action on behalf of justice is integral to the preaching of the Gospel, then action on behalf of women, as well as on behalf of people of color, the poor, and all other oppressed groups is the work of the whole Church.

The importance of this increasing explicitness about the Gospel character of the feminism of committed Catholic women is that it is mainstreaming feminism in the Church. No longer do such feminist Catholics see themselves as pursuing a private women's agenda, a secular project in the Church, or an "extracurricular" activity alongside "real" Church involvement; they now see themselves as acting in the heart of the Church as Jesus the liberator calls them to act and because he calls them to act. It is no accident that Mary Magdalene has been claimed ever more enthusiastically in recent years as the patron of feminists in the Church. She was commissioned by the Risen Jesus to announce the Gospel in the new-born community of the Church, as women are called to do today. The feminist message itself is a contemporary incarnation of the Gospel. This realization is a primary source of resistance to the attempt by some ecclesiastical officials to delegitimate the feminist endeavor as un- or even anti-Christian or as a distraction from the concern of the Church with the poor.

Another major development within the Church that has implications for Catholic feminism is the continuing *emergence of the laity in ministry.* Although this move-ment, at least in its modern form, has its roots in Council documents—the Dogmatic Constitution on the Church *(Lumen Gentium),* the Church in the Modern World *(Gaudium et Spes),* and the Apostolate of Lay People *(Apostolicam Actuositatem)*[13]—it has been undergoing painful purification within the last twenty years, as the retrenchment agenda of the current papacy has attempted to re-clericalize ecclesial ministry.[14] The rap-idly decreasing number of priests and the sexual abuse scandal undermining the credibility of those who remain are making lay ecclesial ministry increasingly necessary for even the day-to-day functioning of ordinary parishes. And as lay ministers—properly prepared, duly installed, and given real responsibility and authority—become more prevalent and more prominent, the body of the faithful is becoming more accustomed to, less resistant to, and more appreciative of this lay incarnation of ecclesial ministry. Women are the majority of these ministers. People are seeing these women in roles they formerly associated with priesthood and therefore exclusively with men. The number of Catholics who say they would be comfortable with women priests continues to rise, due not only to changing minds about women in the abstract but also to changing experiences of real women in ministry.

As mentioned at the outset, the clergy sexual abuse scandal has undermined in a significant way the unexamined equation of priesthood (and thus sacralized maleness) with moral superiority. As men-in-ministry are seen more realistically as human beings rather than epiphanies of the divine, it is easier to see women as potentially and really women-in-ministry. But perhaps a more important result of the scandal is to be seen in the steadfastness of Catholics in their faith despite their disillusionment with the clergy and the hierarchy. As Catholics in the 1960s learned to stand on their own moral feet in the face of *Humanae Vitae,* no longer equating what "the Holy Father said" with the morally good, so Catholics in the first years of the twenty-first century are learning to stand on their own ecclesial feet, no longer equating "father" with the Church. And women are strengthened in their resolve to resist equating their experience of oppression and exclusion by the hierarchy with rejection of their gifts by "the Church" or, even worse, by Jesus or God.[15]

This very brief scan of developments since the first publication of *Beyond Patching* leads me once again to affirm that the threadbare and faded cloak of patriarchy is no longer adequate clothing for the Body of Christ. It is simply "beyond patching" and must be, once and for all, abandoned. It cannot be restored, or transformed, or recycled. Its time is past. But even more so than in 1990, I would want to claim that we are moving, slowly but surely, beyond the futile attempt to patch up the irredeemable and into the more foundational (or radical) task of genuine ecclesial reform. History, the Gospel, and Jesus are on the side of justice and dignity for all God's people, that is, in favor of the Reign of God. If this little book can still help to initiate people into the conversation about faith and feminism in the Church and encourage commitment to Gospel feminism, this new edition will have well repaid the efforts of its author.

Sandra M. Schneiders, IHM
Feast of St. Clare
August 11, 2003

Notes to the Preface

1. It is important to realize that the sexual transgressions of the clergy did not begin in the United States in the 1990s. Women and children have been victimized by male celibates for centuries, but the ecclesiastical conspiracy of secrecy that has been torn open by secular forces in our own day has shielded the offenders while blaming the victims. This conspiracy of silence has been analyzed well by Donald Cozzens in *Sacred Silence: Denial and the Crisis in the Church* (Collegeville, MN: Liturgical Press, 2002). It is also important not to separate the scandal of clerical rape of women Religious in Africa, which began to come to light in the 1990s, from other forms of power-based patriarchal sexual domination. Patriarchy, in other words, is a pervasive ideology that expresses itself in many forms regardless of country, age, sex, ethnicity, or color of the victims.

2. For a brief treatment of and further references to romantic or cultural feminism, see chapter 1. The term "dual anthropology" refers to the understanding of males and females as two types of human being, rather than two ways of realizing a common and shared humanity. It is the basis of the complementarity argument which, in principle, claims that both men and women are "incomplete" without the other, but in practice,

sees men as complete, autonomous, and independent, and women as incomplete, relative, and dependent. Thus it supplies a seemingly irrefutable argument for women's inferiority and subordination to men.

3. The most accessible treatment of the meaning and contours of postmodernity I have found is that of Paul Lakeland, *Postmodernity: Christian Identity in a Fragmented Age* (Minneapolis: Fortress Press, 1997).

4. For a good, brief explanation of the difference between the medieval and modern worldviews, see David Ray Griffin, *God and Religion in the Postmodern World: Essays in Postmodern Theology* (Albany, NY: State University of New York Press, 1989), 13-27.

5. The current shake-up of theology in response to the "new cosmology" or the "universe story" is a very good example of this controlling influence of science. See, for example, Ian G. Barbour, *Religion in an Age of Science,* The Gifford Lectures 1989-1991, vol. 2 (San Francisco: Harper & Row, 1990) and John F. Haught, *God After Darwin: A Theology of Evolution* (Boulder, CO: Westview Press, 2000).

6. For a brief description and criticism of modernity emphasizing its structure and limitations, see Douglas C. Bowman, *Beyond the Modern Mind: The Spiritual and Ethical Challenge of the Environmental Crisis* (New York: Pilgrim Press, 1990), 7-23.

7. For an accessible treatment of the implications of postmodernism for Christian faith, see Stanley J. Grenz, *A Primer on Postmodernism* (Grand Rapids, MI: William B. Eerdmans, 1996).

8. I have explored this development in the academy in much greater detail in *With Oil in Their Lamps: Faith, Feminism, and the Future,* 2000 Madeleva Lecture in Spirituality (New York: Paulist Press, 2000).

9. A very good exposure to the groundbreaking work of Catholic feminist theologians is Catherine Mowry LaCugna, editor, *Freeing Theology: The Essentials of Theology in Feminist Perspective* (San Francisco: Harper, 1993).

10. Lisa Sowle Cahill in "On Being a Catholic Feminist," *The Santa Clara Lectures,* vol. 9, no. 3 (April 27, 2003), 12–18, gives a very good overview of the impact of globalization on Catholic feminism as well as further bibliography on the subject.

11. *The Madeleva Manifesto: A Message of Hope and Courage,* formulated and signed by all the Madeleva lecturers, is promulgated by and available from the Center for Spirituality, Saint Mary's College, Notre Dame, Indiana.

12. "Justice in the World" from the 1971 Synod of Bishops is available in English in *Renewing the Earth: Catholic Documents on Peace, Justice and Liberation,* edited by David J. O'Brien and Thomas A. Shannon (Garden City, NY: Doubleday, 1977), 390–408. The sentence cited is in the Introduction.

13. These documents are available in English in Austin P. Flannery, editor, *Vatican Council II: The Conciliar and Postconciliar Documents,* 2 vols. (Grand Rapids, MI: Eerdmans, 1975 and 1984).

14. A good summary of the current understanding and situation of lay ministry in the United States is Jeffrey Kaster, "Called, Gifted and Now Certified," *America* 189 (July 21–28, 2003), 17–19.

15. On the experience of creative and faithful dissent in the contemporary Church, see Michele Dillon, *Catholic Identity: Balancing Reason, Faith, and Power* (Cambridge, UK: Cambridge University Press, 1999).

Acknowledgements

Books, as any author knows, do not spring into being full grown, like Athena from the mind of Zeus. A written work, though produced by one person, represents the convergence of many beneficent influences and it is my privilege to acknowledge those which have been most important to me in the writing of this book.

First, I would like to thank President Wilfred Murchland, CSC, Dean Ronald Rolheiser, OMI, and the faculty and student body of Newman Theological College in Edmonton, Alberta, Canada for the invitation to deliver the 1990 Anthony Jordan Annual Lectures in Theology of which the chapters in this book are an expanded version. Archbishop Jordan, founder of Newman Theological College, had the foresight and courage to open the doors of the school, once a seminary, to religious and lay women and men responding to the widening understanding of Christian life and ministry after Vatican II. The college continues to honor his memory by engaging in thoughtful exploration of frontier questions in theology by means of the annual Jordan Lectures. It was a privilege to participate in the 1990 celebration.

This invitation to prepare the lectures coincided with a research and writing sabbatical offered to me by my own institution, the Jesuit School of Theology in

Berkeley, California. I am grateful to President Thomas Gleeson, SJ, and Dean David Stagaman, SJ, for providing the respite from regular faculty duties that allowed me to reflect and write.

The material in Chapter 1 on feminism depends not only on the scholars who are cited in the notes but also on the interaction I have enjoyed with feminist women scholars over the last ten years. I mention with particular appreciation and affection Professors Anne Brotherton, SFCC, Joann Wolski Conn, Mary Ann Donovan, SC, Elizabeth Johnson, CSJ, Alice Laffey, Mary Milligan, RSHM, and Kristin Wenzel, OSU. I am grateful to the members of the Women's Initiative in Theology, a project of the Adrian Dominicans and the Sisters, Servants of the Immaculate Heart of Mary, for stimulating exchange at our annual meetings.

Chapter 2 on feminist biblical interpretation had its roots in a seminar on this subject that I taught in 1987 at the Graduate Theological Union in Berkeley, and I gratefully acknowledge the stimulation provided by the interest and enthusiasm of the graduate students, women and men, who participated in the seminar. In 1988 I had three occasions to pursue my research on the topic of feminism and biblical interpretation: the invitation to deliver the Graduate Theological Union Annual Distinguished Faculty Lecture, an invitation to address the Catholic Biblical Association at its annual meeting, and the presidential address to the Society of Biblical Literature Pacific Coast Region. I am grateful for the lively discussion with colleagues that these events occasioned and for the resultant refinement of my own ideas on feminist biblical hermeneutics.

Chapter 3 on feminist spirituality owes a great deal to my experience with women, especially women religious, through participation in colloquia, conventions, chapter preparation events, retreats, and other dialogues in which we have tried to see our way through the suffering and to find energy and courage to meet the challenges of being women in the church today. I acknowledge with special reverence and gratitude the many women I have had the privilege of accompanying in spiritual direction who have shared with me their own faith journeys and especially their deep pain as they have come to feminist consciousness in a patriarchal church. Friends who have been particularly important for my understanding of different dimensions of feminist spirituality are my sister and colleague, Mary Schneiders, OP, Clare Ronzani, SNDdeN, Margaret Goldsbury, CND, Kathleen O'Brien, IHM, and Mary Ann Finch.

I am grateful to the leaders and members of my own religious congregation, especially our president, Dorothy McDaniel, and the members of our provincial team, Eileen Semonin, Helen Schondell, and Catherine Mary Zacharias, who offer me unfailing personal and material support in my theological work.

I am especially grateful to my research assistant, Susan Hames, CSJ, a doctoral student in Christian spirituality whose personal interest in feminist spirituality has been an encouragement, whose knowledge of the field has been a valuable resource, and whose assistance with the actual research was complemented by meticulous attention to the production of the manuscript itself. My thanks also to Robert Stewart, OFM, who helped me with the complexities of the computer and thus greatly eased the final steps of the project.

Although all of the people named above and others who are not named have contributed in important ways to my thinking about the subject matter of this book, responsibility for the final product rests necessarily with me. My hopes are modest enough: that this essay will contribute to the clarity of the conversation about feminism in the church and therefore to progress toward the full inclusion of women in the church of Jesus Christ.

Sandra M. Schneiders, IHM
April 29, 1990
Feast of St. Catherine of Siena
Doctor of the Church

Introduction

In the last thirty years the volume of research and writing about feminism, feminist theology, feminist biblical interpretation, and feminist spirituality has increased with such speed that it has become virtually impossible for any one person to control the field of feminist religious studies. This not only poses a problem for the feminist scholar who wishes to stay current in the field but it also discourages the beginner who cannot discover any expeditious way into the material. Furthermore, the terminology in the field is not only developing very rapidly but different feminist scholars use the same terminology in different ways, making it difficult for the non-specialist to follow a conversation on the subject.

Despite these very real problems an increasing number of scholars in the various branches of religious studies and theology have begun to realize that feminist scholarship is no longer the optional, if not marginal, interest of a few women in the academy. Feminist studies are a necessary complement to and criticism of the heretofore unconsciously masculinized theological enterprise.

Feminist theological scholarship complements traditional theology by raising to visibility that part of Christian history and experience which has been almost completely overlooked or deliberately silenced in the course of the development of the theological tradition, namely the experience and contribution of women. Feminism represents a profound criticism of every aspect of theology: the content of the theological canon including both scripture and tradition, the subject matter and arguments of classical theology, and the masculinized methods of the discipline.

Obviously, in the scope of a small book we cannot even begin to discuss the feminist theological agenda, to expose its contributions, or to evaluate its criticism. Indeed, I do not consider myself competent to undertake such a comprehensive presentation even if there were space for it here. The purpose of this little volume is much more modest, namely to provide the tools necessary for the theologically literate (though not necessarily specialist) reader to undertake at his or her own pace an investigation of feminist theological thought.

I want, first of all, to explain the basic vocabulary of the field, indicating where there is general agreement about terminology and ideas and where there is substantial disagreement. This fundamental definitional and descriptive project is undertaken in the first chapter.

In the second chapter I attempt a preliminary approach to what I consider the most fundamental theological problem raised by the feminist critique: how scripture, once its androcentric, patriarchal, and misogynist content has been identified, can function normatively for Christians, especially for women. This question is fundamental because for Christians the touchstone not only of theology but of faith itself is the Bible understood as word of God. Unless we can find a way to understand scripture which denies neither its normative status in the community of faith nor the very real problems raised by its sometimes morally unacceptable treatment of women, the foundations of Christian faith itself are fatally undermined.

Finally, in the third chapter I turn to the actual experience of women Christians, especially Catholics, whose feminist consciousness has been raised and who, consequently, find themselves in excruciating tension with the institutional church and even with Christian faith as it is articulated and practiced within the believing community. Women who are both Christian and feminist face not only theological problems but also, and especially, problems in the area of spirituality, i.e. in their lived experience of the faith. These problems are numerous and deep. What is one to do when the male God-image that nourished one's faith from infancy to adulthood becomes at best incredible and at worst oppressive? How is one to relate to a male savior who represents a male God who is invoked to legitimate the claim that maleness is normative for humanity? Where does one turn when sacraments have ceased to mediate the encounter with God because they are experienced as instruments for a sacralized subjugation of women believers by male clerics? What does one do with the endless and exhausting rage that is called forth by sexual apartheid in the church, by ubiquitous linguistic sexism, by clerical monopoly of ministry, by blatantly oppressive liturgy? These and related issues have stimulated the development of feminist spirituality which is actually a multiform phenomenon. Without attempting an exhaustive analysis or evaluation of the phenomenon, I have tried to describe feminist spirituality, to distinguish its major manifestations in their similarity, variety, and relationships, and to suggest the significance of this development for the church.

In short, this slim volume attempts to offer the reader a primer on feminism, feminist theology, and feminist spirituality which will enable her or him to enter into the feminist conversation with a basic grasp of the vocabulary, agenda, and underlying assumptions of the feminist movement as it touches the faith and life of the believer.

I am convinced that the dialogue between feminism and

the church is not only important and timely, but absolutely critical. Crisis is a situation of danger and opportunity. The citation from Mark which supplied the title for this book captures well the danger. The seamless garment of the body of Christ, an ancient image of the unity of the church, has grown old, thin, and faded. The sins of patriarchy, notably sexism, clericalism, and racism, have created great tears in the fabric of unity. Some in the church would like to see feminism as a patch which can be sewn, inconspicuously they hope, over the rips and tears of division. But those who would reduce feminism to a local repair job on an otherwise still usable garment risk aggravating rather than improving the situation. Feminism is not a patch; it is a whole new pattern which can only be realized by weaving a new garment, seamless from top to bottom and multicolored from the beginning. The title *Beyond Patching* is deliberately ambiguous. By it I want to suggest, first of all, that the old garment is beyond repair and that only a thoroughgoing reform of the church can respond adequately to the feminist critique.

No doubt such a project is frightening to those who still equate the garment of monochromatic masculinism with the unity of the church. Without doubt the project is difficult and costly. But the feminist crisis presents the church also with opportunity, the historical possibility of putting off the old garment of oppressive domination, of moving beyond patching, in order to put on the radiant new wedding garment that is required for the eschatological banquet.

1

Feminism: Women's Fad or Humanity's Future?

I. Introduction

Most people understand the term "feminism" sufficiently well to react viscerally when it is used. But if asked to define the term, much less come to agreement with others about what it means or designates, they often find themselves reduced to vague generalities. This situation is easily explained by the fact that, on the one hand, there is extreme theoretical and practical diversity within the feminist movement and among feminists themselves while, on the other hand, there is a family resemblance among feminists, even those who represent the most diverse types of feminist thought and styles of feminist commitment.

In the face of such a situation one is tempted to shrug one's mental shoulders and blandly agree that feminism is whatever feminists think and do and feminists are those who claim to be. I do not think such intellectual defeatism is necessary or wise because, whatever else feminism may be, it is a powerful worldwide phenomenon which is deeply affecting all social reality.[1] Pope John XXIII, in his 1963 encyclical *Pacem in Terris,* linked the emergence of women into public life with the rise of the working class and the emergence of new nations as one of the "distinctive characteristics" of our age, a "sign of the times" to which we must attend if we are effectively to live and preach the gospel in the twentieth century.[2] Therefore, it would seem that it is worth our while to try to understand the nature and goals of feminism because only such understanding will enable us to carry on meaningful conversations about this world-transforming movement and to make responsible decisions about our own participation in its agenda. Our first task, then, is to achieve at least a basic understanding of feminism as the foundation for a discussion of Christian feminism and finally of Christian feminist spirituality.

II. Mapping the Linguistic Terrain

Although there is no universal agreement among feminists on the vocabulary of feminism I think it is possible to map the linguistic terrain with enough accuracy that first-time visitors to the area can orient themselves and more experienced travelers can recognize their positions. I will begin by defining three terms which are fairly basic and about which there is considerable agreement, mainly because they are defined historically rather then ontologically: women's movement, women's emancipation movement, and women's liberation movement.

Women's movement is probably the widest term and can be applied to a large number of movements throughout history which were born in the collective realization by some women that they were disadvantaged in relation to men within their particular familial, cultural, social, or religious settings. This realization led to some kind of organized action by these women to better their situation or to right the perceived wrongs. Many of these women's movements, especially those predating the nineteenth century, would not be considered feminist movements[3] because those who engaged in them were not motivated by what has come to be called "feminist consciousness," i.e. by an awareness of the systemic and structural character of women's oppression and a commitment not merely to obtaining redress of grievances but to the structural transformation of society.[4]

However, the term "women's movement" is usually used today to denote the widespread social and political stirring of women, first in Europe in the late nineteenth century, then in the United States at the beginning of the twentieth century, and finally increasingly in third world countries in our own day. This modern women's movement is feminist in the technical sense of the word, and this accounts for the understandable tendency to use the two terms, women's movement and feminism, interchangeably. It is useful, nevertheless, to distinguish between them because there are contemporary women's movements, i.e. organized collective efforts by women to further their own interests, which feminists in general would repudiate precisely because these women define their own interests in patriarchal terms.[5]

Our second term, *women's emancipation,* is narrower in application than women's movement and usually denotes, at least in the United States, the movement for women's political and legal equality which began in the first decade of this century and whose "first wave" culminated in 1920 with the ratification of the nineteenth amendment to the U.S. Constitution giving women the right to vote.[6] The primary objective of this movement, as its name indicates, was the freeing of women from their status as political minors. The right to vote made women adult participants in the republic. However, just as the Emancipation Proclamation which freed the slaves did not achieve equality for blacks in this country, so suffrage did not achieve equality for women. What it did was create the fundamental structural possibility for women's achieving equality, a process that is still far from complete. The "second wave" of this process began in the 1960s, at the same time and fueled by the same energies as the civil rights movement and the anti-war movement, and it is embodied most visibly today in the effort to obtain ratification for the Equal Rights Amendment.[7]

The women's emancipation movement was, from the beginning, explicitly feminist in that those who struggled for women's suffrage, even though not all had exactly the same motivation, were all motivated by the conviction that according women the vote established the possibility of changing the basic structures of society in the direction of justice. For some women the structures that needed changing were those which excluded women from full adult participation in political life. For others, the structures that needed changing were slavery, child labor, and the threat to the family represented by male alcoholism, all of which, these women believed, they would be able to change once they could vote. Thus, both those who espoused full political and legal equality for women and those who would never have voted for such a radical and widespread change in social arrangements could come together on the limited issue of suffrage. Such unity has not been achieved in regard to the Equal Rights Amendment[8] which was introduced into Congress just three years after the ratification of the nineteenth amendment and which has still not been ratified, due largely to opposition from women who do not equate women's rights with equal rights. We will return to this point later.

Our third term, *women's liberation,* is much broader than women's emancipation and is the form that the women's movement in this country took as the so-called "second wave" developed in the 1960s.[9] The women's liberation movement is not only explicitly feminist in that it arises from a developed feminist consciousness, but it is much more inclusive in its agenda than was the women's emancipation movement of the early 1900s. The liberation which contemporary feminists seek is not merely freedom *from* marginalization, oppression, discrimination, and violence but freedom *for* self-definition, self-affirmation, and self-determination; in other words, the effective recognition of their full humanity as persons and the freedom to exercise that personhood in every sphere. Thus, the contemporary movement envisions not only political and legal rights for women equal to those of men but the liberation of women (and men) into the fullness of human personhood. This liberation will require not merely the reform of current societal arrangements but a total transformation of ideology and structures, a reimagining of personal and social reality that will leave no person, group, or institution unchanged.

If these three terms are fairly easy to define because they refer to recognizable historical movements, there are two correlated terms crucial to an understanding of feminism which are much disputed, namely, equality and rights. The basic reason for the deep divisions not only between feminists and non-feminists but also among feminists themselves around these concepts is that women as an oppressed group are unlike any other oppressed class. While women are the most oppressed in every class to which they belong, they do not really constitute *a* class as such. Women belong to every class, including oppressor classes such as whites or the wealthy. What women have in common is not class but sex, and sex is not, like skin color, ethnic origin, language, age, or economic status, either irrelevant in the area of rights or remediable. Skin color is irrelevant and poverty is remediable. But sex is neither and most feminists do not want to argue otherwise.

What women have in common across all class lines, and

that which is the basis of their oppression, is femaleness defined in opposition to maleness and that means essentially in terms of women's different role in reproduction.[10] This puts women in a "Catch-22." To argue that femaleness is not really different in any significant way from maleness and therefore that there is no basis for differential treatment of women (the absolute equal rights argument) is to surrender precisely what women have come to value, namely their unique worth as women which grounds their specific and irreplaceable contribution to the human enterprise including but by no means limited to their preponderant role in procreation.

However, to accept that there is a real difference between women and men and that that difference is based on sexuality is to open women to the arguments for defining women in terms of gender, (something never done in regard to men as men who are always defined in terms of their humanity), reducing women to their reproductive identity and roles, and thus limiting women's rights, denying them equality, and in general affirming their current structural oppression because they are something other than and therefore less than simply human.

This dilemma is sometimes referred to as the problem of "sameness versus difference."[11] The question becomes: Is women's agenda better furthered by insisting on the humanity which women share with men (sameness) or on their femaleness which is not equatable to maleness (difference)? Should women be struggling for human rights or for women's rights?[12] And does not the very acceptance of that distinction constitute acceptance of the equation of male with human and thus the definition of non-childbearing maleness as the norm for humanity from which women diverge in giving life?

The term "equal rights" muddies the water even more

because, in liberation movements in general, equal rights means rights for the oppressed equal to those enjoyed by the oppressor, e.g. rights for blacks equal to those enjoyed by whites. But in the case of women, because male has been equated with human, equal rights and human rights both amount to male rights for women. Thus, the very attaining of equal rights constitutes an acceptance of the normativity of the male, an admission that the best way to be a woman, because it is the only way to be fully human, is to be like a man.[13] Obviously, this is not acceptable to most feminists.

A final complication of this whole issue is introduced by the difference between the Anglo-American and other political traditions. In the Anglo-American tradition the individual is the basic unit of society and the personal subject of inalienable rights. Thus, the argument is that human rights are individual rights of the person, regardless of sex. However, in many other cultures the family, either nuclear as in Europe or extended as in many third world countries, is regarded as the basic unit of society. In these cultures there is a strong tendency to understand women's rights as complementary to men's rights within the relational unity of the family.[14] Women's rights are then closely related to their different role in procreation, i.e. to motherhood, which is therefore the legitimate basis for special claims.

Such an understanding of women's rights can lead to a strong feminist position which rejects any domination of women by men or societal discrimination against women while insisting that society be structured to foster and respect women's special role in the procreative process. However, it can also lead both to the romantic exaltation of womanhood in the "feminine mystique" with its ideology of complementarity and to the legitimation of the definition of women in reproductive terms and their consequent limitation to the private domain of home and family. Thus, many American

Roman Catholic feminists find papal documents on women such as John Paul II's recent *Mulieres Dignitatem*[15] to be distressing examples of an unhealthy and unrealistic romanticizing of womanhood as motherhood combined with complementarity arguments for denying women their proper role as adults in society and as baptized Christians in the church. However, the basic type of argumentation embodied in the papal document, although not necessarily its discriminatory conclusions, would find acceptance among some feminists whose credentials are impeccable.[16] In other words, not all relational feminism is romantic and not all individualist feminism is unisex. But relational feminism, especially in a patriarchal culture, is particularly susceptible to identifying with male circumscriptions of women's personhood in terms of gender and reproductive function; and individualist feminism, especially in an androcentric society, is particularly susceptible to accepting the equation of maleness and male rights with humanity and human rights.

In my opinion, any solution to this complicated dilemma will have to incorporate two basic tenets. First, it must eschew both unisex denials of women's uniqueness and complementarity as a model for male-female relations. Second, it will have to embrace both individual rights and relational responsibilities for both men and women on the basis of the self-definition and self-determination of both, not the self-determination of men and the male definition of women.

First, feminists of all persuasions are becoming increasingly convinced that the cause of women is ill-served by denying the differences between women and men and that, beyond ensuring the dignity and safety of women against male oppression and abuse, feminism is committed to enabling women to make their specific contribution as women to the entire human enterprise. Humanity will not be fully human until women contribute as women and as equals with men to its definition and its realization. However, whatever may be said for complementarity as a theoretical position, it is politically non-viable. While it may be argued that women and men "complete" one another, at least in the area of reproduction, the term complete has never meant the same thing for women as for men. Women have been seen to complete men the way a second coat of paint completes a house, whereas men have been seen to complete women the way a motor completes a car. In other words, completion can be accidental or essential, and there is probably no way to rescue the category of complementarity from its historical bias toward seeing women as decorations or adjuncts to the essentially self-sufficient male considered as normative human being.

Second, both women and men are the subjects of individual rights and both have relational responsibilities. The system of ascribing individual rights to men and then granting to women, by way of privilege, only those rights which do not conflict with what men regard as women's relational responsibilities cannot be accepted. In most respects and in the vast majority of situations the individual humanity of men and women is identical and equal rights are, indeed, identical rights. However, in those areas in which the differences between men and women are real and significant, justice requires structures that ensure individuals equitable rather than identical opportunity and access to society's resources and advantages. Thus, since women alone bear children, the economic structures of society must ensure that this unique contribution to the good of society does not disadvantage women. On the other hand, men have exactly the same responsibilities as women do to raise the children they engender, and economic structures must recognize the equal obligations of both parents and ensure that both have equal opportunities to fulfill their responsibilities. In other words, where the natural situation is not identical, equity must insure substantial equality. Where the natural situation is identical, patriarchal definitions of humanity must not create disadvantages for women.

The obstacle to realizing such a just social arrangement is that men have enjoyed, from time immemorial, a position of dominance from which they could define women as not only different from themselves but as inferior on the basis of that difference. For example, since men cannot bear children they have defined childlessness as normal and normative, set up the work structure for this "normal" situation, and made childbearing a medical condition, i.e. an illness, and therefore an obstacle to full employment and advancement. Because men, as a group, have never accepted their equal parental responsibility, they are under the illusion that not caring daily for one's children is normal and have structured the economic situation for "normal" people, that is, for those without child care responsibilities. Only when women contribute equally with men to the definition of humanity will it be realized that what is normal for women is normal for humanity just as what is normal for men is normal for humanity. Just and equitable structuring of society requires that the needs, responsibilities, and opportunities of all members of society are equally respected and provided for, not that all members of society be identical or be treated identically.

In short, the struggle for equal rights must not be abandoned. But equal rights must be redefined in terms of equity rather than identity. This struggle will probably have to be carried out through the judicial process of interpreting a fundamental Equal Rights Amendment that establishes the basic principle of equality,[17] analogous to the way judicial interpretation has had to determine progressively, as new situations arise, the meaning of separation of church and state on the basis of the first amendment's fundamental guarantee of religious liberty. At the same time, however, the struggle for women's liberation cannot be reduced to the struggle for equal rights even if the term equal rights is properly understood. The final goal of women's liberation is a human social order in which women are fully self-determining, fully participating members. Such a society is not one in which women have whatever men have decided is good for women or even what men have decided is good for men, but in which both women and men enjoy the conditions necessary for the exercise of full human personhood.

III. Feminism

Against the background of these terminological clarifications we can approach our original question "What is feminism?" with a more grounded hope of reaching some clarity. I will propose a basic definition of feminism and then try, by explaining its components, to describe the phenomenon more fully. Feminism, I would propose, is a comprehensive ideology which is rooted in women's experience of sexual oppression, engages in a critique of patriarchy as an essentially dysfunctional system, embraces an alternative vision for humanity and the earth, and actively seeks to bring this vision to realization.[18]

A. A Comprehensive Ideology

The first component of our definition is the classification of feminism as an ideology. It is not ideology negatively understood as a mindset and system of values uncritically absorbed from one's cultural context, or as false consciousness in the Freudian or Marxist senses of the term. Rather, it is ideology in two of the senses given in Webster's Third Unabridged Dictionary: "a systematic scheme or *coordinated*

body of ideas or concepts, esp. about human life or culture"
and "the integrated assertions, theories, and aims that constitute a *sociopolitical program."* In other words, feminism is
a comprehensive theoretical system for analyzing, criticizing,
and evaluating ideas, social structures, procedures and practices, indeed the whole of experienced reality. But it is more
than a theoretical system for criticism because it involves the
proposal of an alternative vision and a commitment to bringing that vision to socio-political realization. This definition of
feminism as an ideology suggests immediately that one cannot be a feminist by default, e.g. by not being overtly and
deliberately sexist; or anonymously, i.e. without knowing it;
or on the side, as an interest which can be displaced in favor
of other concerns.[19]

B. Rooted in an Experience of Sexual Oppression

The second component of the definition is that feminism is rooted in an experience of sexual oppression. Feminism, although it is an ideology, i.e. a theoretical system,
does not begin in theory but in experience. Consciousness
raising or conscientization is the process by which one becomes aware, first, that one's negative experience is due to
oppression rather than to personal failure; second, that the
oppression is structural rather than fortuitous or incidental.
This raised consciousness becomes feminist consciousness
when one recognizes that this structural oppression is based
on sex, i.e. that one is being oppressed because one is a
woman in a system controlled by men for their own advantage. Finally, one becomes aware that one is not an isolated
victim but that one belongs to an oppressed group which, if
it can convert its solidarity in oppression into solidarity in
action, can change the oppressive structures.[20]

By way of example, a divorced mother whose ex-husband has vanished, defaulting permanently on alimony and child support, and who cannot get a job because she cannot afford day care for her child, blames herself as a failure, a social incompetent who just cannot "make it" in a system that seems to work for everyone else. Through a process of consciousness raising she begins to see that what seemed to be her personal problems are actually systemically generated problems.[21] There is a close interconnection between legal tolerance of paternal financial abandonment, cultural expectations that the mother will assume total responsibility for child rearing, social refusal to develop an adequate and effective child care system, and economic structuring of gainful employment so that only those without child rearing responsibilities can participate competently. In short, there is no way she can "make it" in the system no matter how hard she tries because the system has been structured to exclude and defeat her. She also becomes aware that all of these structural factors in her apparent inability to function competently in society affect her because she is a woman. And, finally, she comes to realize that she is not alone. The system does not, in fact, work for "everyone else" but only for males and those women whose situation resembles that of males. At this point the woman has developed a feminist consciousness, a process some prominent feminist theorists such as Letty Russell, Beverly Wildung Harrison, Rosemary Radford Ruether, and Sheila Collins have not hesitated to call a "conversion."

Consciousness raising, the critical appropriation of personal experience as systemic oppression, has been encapsulated in a phrase that some have called the analytical nerve of feminism, namely "the personal is political." The most basic meaning of this phrase is that what women have been taught to experience as "personal problems" are not personal or private but are generated by the social systems within which women live.[22] Therefore, they cannot be solved by making psychological or spiritual adjustments in one's personal life, however important such personal transformation may be, but only by the transformation of socio-political reality.[23] On the other hand, social transformation demands personal transformation through consciousness raising, bonding with others, and accessing one's personal power. This process of personal transformation has come to be called feminist spirituality, a topic we will take up in Chapter 3. The point here is that there is an intrinsic and reciprocal relationship between personal transformation and societal transformation. Feminist consciousness leads necessarily to socio-political involvement, and socio-political transformation demands and facilitates personal transformation.[24] We find the same intrinsic connection between spirituality and social justice involvement in the feminist movement that we find in other liberation movements such as those in Latin America or among American blacks.

C. Critique of Patriarchy

The third element in our definition of feminism is its critique of patriarchy. All forms of feminism recognize that patriarchy is a basic cause of women's oppression.[25] However, the approach a feminist takes to patriarchy, how patriarchy is defined, and the role it is believed to play in both social organization as a whole and the oppression of women in particular, will place a given feminist within one of the main categories of contemporary feminism, namely liberal, cultural, socialist (including Marxist), or radical feminism.[26]

Liberal feminism is predominantly concerned with the political and legal situation of women in society, and its major goal is the achieving of equal rights for women within the prevailing socio-political system. The liberal definition of patriarchy is functionally synonymous with sexism in practice, i.e. with the discriminatory attitudes and practices by which men oppress women, especially as these are embodied in social, political, and economic structures.

Cultural feminism is sometimes called romantic or social reform feminism. It is concerned with what it regards as the special contributions of women to the construction of a better world. Often cultural feminists, both men and women, regard women as having a certain intrinsic moral superiority to men. Women are peace-makers, egalitarians, less ambitious and driven, more person oriented, more cooperative, less competitive, more nurturing, and so on, than men are. Cultural feminists tend to define patriarchy as the exclusive triumph of male values in culture, and their concern is the equal and mutual influence of men and women in the transformation of culture.

Most American feminists, with the exception of the conservative pro-family group that has emerged in the last few years,[27] would certainly support the liberal feminist agenda of equal rights and opportunities for women. Furthermore, the rhetoric and values of cultural feminism often permeate the discourse and the action agenda of other feminist groups. However, both socialist and radical feminists regard the social analysis of liberal and cultural feminists as inadequate. Liberal feminists do not really question the capitalist system; they basically want women to be free to participate in it as equals with men. Cultural feminists do question the system, but their fundamental concern is not to remake the socio-politico-economic order but to humanize the system by infusing into it the heretofore unheard voice and values of the female half of the human race.

The feminism with which I am primarily concerned is that which has done a deep analysis of contemporary social reality and which envisions its total transformation. Socialist and radical feminism have this perspective and agenda in common. They differ, however, in their conclusions about the precise nature and role of patriarchy in the current construction of reality and therefore on strategy for dealing with it.

The Marxist influence in **socialist feminism** leads its adherents to see the economic class structure, based on relationship to the means of production, as the fundamental structure of oppression in society. Socialist feminists define patriarchy as a set of social relations among men which is supported and maintained by their control over women. "It recognizes a system of hierarchy among men drawn along race and class lines, but argues that the common goal of the control of women unites all men beyond race and class."[28] In other words, sexual economics rooted in the division of labor by gender that assigns the private sphere of reproduction to women and the public sphere of production to men rather than sexual identity or role in the family unit is the root of the problem, the ultimate explanation of male domination and oppression of women.

Maria Riley argues that socialist feminism is the most comprehensive form of feminist analysis since it attempts to explain the interrelations among all forms of oppression, viz. sexual, racial, and economic.[29] Its analysis finally locates the root of all oppressions in the economic sphere. The development of capitalist class society entails the subordination of women and their reproductive capacity to the control of the owners of the means of production, viz. men. Thus males constitute a dominant class within every class, and this intraclass domination has the same structure as the overall interclass structure of society in that it is based on the control by some, for their own advantage, of the productive capacity of others. Sexism, then, is a subset of classism which is the more comprehensive category, and economics is more basic than sex as the root of oppression, even the oppression of women by men. Patriarchy is an alliance among oppressors across racial and class lines and will ultimately be undone by the abolition of the oppressive and alienating economic system which grounds the classist social order.

Other feminists, however, question the historical validity of the socialist analysis. Black women, for example, often maintain that racial oppression of blacks, both men and women, is more significant and more powerful than any supposed alliance of black men with white men in the oppression of women, even though black feminists are powerful critics of black male oppression of black women.[30]

Gerda Lerner argues that it was not the development of class society based on private property that led to male inclusion of women among their capital possessions but rather that male ownership and control of women's reproductive capacity was the original form of private property. In other words, patriarchy led to capitalism, not the other way around.[31] The abolition of capitalism, therefore, will not liberate women, a conclusion that has certainly been borne out in the Marxist regimes in this century.

Nancy Chodorow, in her first major feminist work,[32] has called the Marxist analysis into question on the basis of cultural and psychological anthropology because she became convinced that the oppression of women well preceded class society. In her most recent book, she questions the Marxist explanation from the standpoint of psychoanalysis which reveals the root of male oppression of women in male fear and hatred of women "because they experience them as powerful mothers."[33] Chodorow wants to move from a single-cause explanation for women's oppression to a complex social, cultural, and psychological explanation.

Radical feminism, like socialist feminism, mounts a thoroughgoing critique of the social system as a whole but evaluates the role of patriarchy within that system differently.

Radical feminism regards patriarchy not merely as a system of male domination of females, and therefore as a subset of the overall problem of class oppression, but as the basic dominative social system which is the ground and paradigm for all forms of social domination. It has the advantage of being based not on an hypothesis about the development of social systems but on verifiable social history. Patriarchy is the social system of father-rule which is the basic form of social organization in every historical society we know anything about, at least in the west. While there seem to have been matrifocal and matrilineal societies, and certainly societies in which the supreme deity was the Great Mother Goddess, there is no hard historical evidence that there has ever been a matriarchal society, i.e. a social system based on mother-rule in which women controlled the religious myth and symbol system.[34]

In this analysis patriarchy or father-rule consists in the ownership by the male head of the household of all persons, land, and resources attached to the household. Thus, in ancient societies, he owned wives and concubines, children, slaves, animals, land, produce, and money and had not only responsibility for his property but also absolute power over it. It was the right of the head of the household to expose unwanted infants; to sell, barter, or donate wives, children, or slaves; to kill recalcitrant dependents; to acquire and alienate real and personal property. This absolute power, including that of life and death, was rooted in his ownership of the household as economic unit, and this ownership was based on his position as *paterfamilias,* male head of the family, clan, or tribe.

While this power belonged to the male head of the household, its exercise was not restricted to control over females. Minor sons who had not yet become heads of their own households, male in-laws if they resided in the house-

hold, and male slaves were as subject to the *patria potestas* as
were women, with the difference that any male could, at least
in principle, attain to full majority whereas women, precisely
because they could never be fathers of families, were minors
by nature. It is not difficult to understand the development of
this form of social organization from the need of the social
unit to protect itself, and particularly to protect the females
whose fertility was the source of the unit's continuance. Nor
is it difficult to understand the assumption that this arrangement was natural, i.e. ordained by divinity and therefore not
subject to human revision. In other words, patriarchy or
father-rule was essentially hierarchy (from *hieros,* sacred) or
divinely sanctioned, sacralized responsibility, authority and
power.

What this analysis of patriarchy makes clear is that patriarchy is not simply the domination of individual women by
individual men. It is a principle and paradigm of social organization which is based not on maleness as such but on
the social role assumed by or assigned to adult male household heads in the structure. Furthermore, the social stratifica-
tion in the system is not based solely on sex. While one could
not be in the dominant position unless one were a male (or
acting in the place of or by permission of a male), one could
be a male and not be in the dominant position. However,
because the role of head of the social unit belonged to the
husband-father who was necessarily male, there was an evident and intrinsic connection established between maleness, property, and power on the one hand and femaleness,
economic dependence, and powerlessness on the other.
Whatever was characterized by dependence and powerlessness came to be associated with the feminine and whatever
was characterized by ownership and power came to be associated with the masculine. Herein we see the root of the
inveterate tendency of the western mind to divide all reality

into gendered dyads, i.e. into opposites assimilated to the male or female pole, and to evaluate each member positively or negatively depending on that assimilation. Mind and body, spirit and matter, culture and nature, life and death, light and darkness, intellect and feeling, reason and intuition, and innumerable other pairs cast all reality into a superior/ inferior, domination/subordination schema.[35] The radical feminist analysis traces all the dominance relations in the social order to the system of universal hierarchical dualism that finds its first and basic instance as well as its paradigm in the dominance/subordination relationship between male household head and wife-mother that is the principle of the patriarchal family unit. In short, patriarchy is not one exam- ple of classism but the root of all hierarchical relationships including not only sexism but also classism, clericalism, colo- nialism, racism, ageism, and heterosexism. While it is not exclusively a male over female structure it is essentially and pervasively sexual, drawing its psychic energy as well as its basic example from the dominance relation of male to fe- male in the familial unit. The pervasive tendency of domi- nators to feminize and/or infantilize the oppressed is no coincidence because the title to dominate comes basically from the assumption or the defense of patriarchal privilege.

Radical feminist analysis, like the socialist feminist anal- ysis, perceives the interconnectedness of all forms of op- pression and draws the necessary conclusion that sexist oppression cannot be overcome unless all forms of domina- tion and oppression are overcome, and this requires the transformation of society literally from the root up. It differs from socialist feminism in identifying patriarchy, rather than economically based classism, as the root that must be healed. The fear of radical feminism that has been expressed with increasing alarm by ecclesiastical officials[36] is actually quite well founded because the Roman Catholic Church, as a social institution, is perhaps the most patriarchal structure in the western world and it has even, at times, defined itself as hierarchical by divine institution. Catholic radical feminists have identified patriarchy in general and hierarchy (i.e. sacralized patriarchy) in particular as an irredeemably sinful structure whose transformation is demanded by the gospel and is the *sine qua non* of the coming of the reign of God which is, by divine institution, not a hierarchy but a discipleship of equals.

D. An Alternative Vision

All forms of feminism have in common the proposal of an alternative vision of life in this world. Liberal feminists envision a social order in which women will have political status and legal rights equal to those of men. Cultural feminists envision a world humanized and enriched by the mutual and equal contributions of women and men to the ideal of humanity and its realization. Socialist feminists dream of a classless society based on non-alienated labor in which sex, race, ethnic origin, and all other distinctions will have become economically and socially irrelevant. In my opinion, radical feminism not only offers the most comprehensive and imaginative vision of an alternative future but also embraces the values espoused by other kinds of feminism. Therefore, I will attempt to sketch the feminist ideal in its terms.

Because radical feminism identifies patriarchy, especially in its sacralized form of hierarchy, as the root of all forms of oppression, the root of its alternative vision is its resolute anti-hierarchicalism, or, to phrase it positively, its fundamental egalitarianism. This egalitarianism is much more comprehensive than equal individual rights, although equal rights are certainly part of the radical feminist agenda. It has to do with the equality of persons as human beings and even a kind of equality among all the orders of being within creation.

Feminist egalitarianism is not a utopian blindness to or denial of real differences but a refusal to dichotomize differences into inferior and superior as bases for domination/ subordination relationships between people or between humans and the rest of creation. Furthermore, egalitarianism is not anti-organizational nor does it deny the necessity and usefulness of leadership. But it believes that order need not involve the subordination of some to others and that leadership does not consist in the exercise of coercive power over others but in the capacity to empower others in the pursuit of freely chosen common goals.

The fundamental repudiation of hierarchy that is at the center of the feminist vision has many corollaries. For example, in the feminist vision competition and its ultimate escalation into war must give way to cooperation and the sharing of resources as the basis of a just and lasting peace; violence and coercion must be replaced by dialogue and consensus building for the resolution of conflicts; the rights of all to participate according to their interests and capacities in all systems and decisions which affect them must be vindicated; inclusion must replace exclusion as the way to maximize power; and humans must begin to see themselves as participants in rather than lords over the fragile ecosystem that is our earth. How to embody this vision in the concrete structures and relationships of everyday life, especially since none of us has much experience of such a non-oppressive relational universe, is a challenge feminists struggle with virtually every time they come together. But the conviction that hierarchy is the root of sinful structures and that it must be eradicated and replaced with an egalitarian vision and praxis if the human family and the earth are to survive and flourish is non-negotiable.

In Chapter 3 we will discuss this vision in greater detail, but what should be obvious at this point is that the alternative vision of radical feminism is not simply a world without sexism, i.e. a world in which men no longer oppress women. Sexism is properly seen as the paradigmatic form of oppression. However, it is not the only form. All oppression is based on dichotomous dualisms. Classism, racism, clericalism, colonialism, heterosexism, ageism, as well as all oppressive forms of government from divine right monarchies to police states, are connected, at their root, by the principle of patriarchy. No form of oppression can be finally overcome until that root is cut, until hierarchy as such is delegitimated and replaced by a universal acceptance of the basic equality of all participants in creation. In other words, in the feminist utopian vision the end of any oppression depends on the end of all oppression because the connection among oppressions is not one of similarity or even of the solidarity in suffering of the victims. It is an ideological connection which involves not only a certain oppressive theory of reality but a praxis which draws its validity from and validates that theory.

E. Realizing the Feminist Future

We come finally to the fifth component in the definition of feminism, the active commitment of feminists to bringing about the incarnation of the feminist vision in the social order. Feminism espouses a utopian vision, but it is not content to dream about an alternative future. However, just as all feminists do not analyze patriarchy in exactly the same way, nor do all have exactly the same vision of an alternative future, so not all feminists choose the same means for achieving that future.

    Maria Riley in her fine volume on feminism and Catholic
social thought speaks of the "carriers" of the vision of various
strands of the feminist movement.[37] Who are the people and
what are the organizations and organs through which various types of feminism work toward the realization of a feminist future? Liberal feminism is perhaps the most visible form
of feminism in the United States precisely because its major
carriers are bureaucratic and organizational agencies such
as the National Organization for Women, the League of
Women Voters, the women's caucuses in legislative bodies,
action organizations among businesswomen, professional
women, and women workers, and women's groups pressing
for change in the church such as the Women's Ordination
Conference and various groups of lay women and women
religious.

    Organizational feminism is highly effective because it
uses the techniques and structures which are already in place
in the dominant society and which people in power understand in order to undermine the patriarchal agenda and
praxis in state and church. The increasing number of women
in elective office, the steady battering down of the doors
which bar women from the networks of power in business
and the professions, the increasing success of women in
legally vindicating their rights against male harassment and
abuse on the street, in the home, and in the workplace, and
the consistent pressure being brought to bear on sexist
policies and practices in the churches are gradually disman-
tling the complex interlocking structures of male power and
privilege.

    Cultural feminism's vision of an alternative future is less
focused on women's attaining of equal rights in society than
on the transforming moral influence of women in a world
suffering from over-masculinization. Cultural feminism is dif-
fused throughout the feminist movement, and its rhetoric

and agenda tend to appear wherever feminists are active. A very interesting contemporary expression of cultural feminism is the Mothers Against Drunk Driving campaign with its highly suggestive acronym, MADD. Not unlike the Women's Temperance Movement at the beginning of the century, MADD is a grassroots movement of women, self-consciously affirming their life-giving identity and role as mothers, enraged at the predominantly male disregard of life, especially the life of these women's children, and determined to do something about it. They do not see themselves primarily or simply as citizens, voters, adults, or even as women or parents, and their target is not irresponsible public behavior as such. They see themselves specifically as mothers taking up arms against the slaughter of their children, and they have identified the culture's macho attitude toward alcohol and cars as the enemy. However, in general, the values of cultural feminism appear less in particular movements or organizations than as the ethos within which the feminist movement in general operates.

Socialist and radical feminism are generally carried by collectivist groups of all sizes and degrees of formal organization rather than by bureaucratic agencies in relation to society's current organizational structure. Socialist feminists tend to target economic and reproductive issues while radical feminists, without neglecting these issues, are primarily concerned with the empowering of women in their struggle against male oppression and the elaboration of an alternative feminist reality.

Radical feminism is the branch of the movement that is most concerned with religion, both religion's role in the subordination of women and religion's potential for liberation. Feminist spirituality, the topic of Chapter 3, is predominantly located within the precincts of radical feminism which is also primarily involved in the construction of alternative places

and agencies for women: women's collectives, support networks for rape victims, safe houses for battered women and
children, counseling services for women involved in family
planning decisions, educational alternatives for women who
find themselves suddenly independent through separation,
divorce, or widowhood, women's support groups in universities, seminaries, parishes, and other male-dominated institutions, feminist prayer and liturgy groups, and numerous
other projects, large and small, in which feminist vision and
values can be incarnated here and now and can demonstrate
the viability and desirability of an alternative future.

Both the socialist and the radical branches of the feminist movement have been deeply involved in the academic
agenda of feminism which calls for a complete revisioning of
western social and intellectual history from which women's
story and contribution have been largely erased.[38] Thus,
women's studies programs in universities, women's caucuses within the major scholarly societies, women's publica-
tions and films, and major feminist research projects of all
kinds are part of the active agenda of the movement.

In summary, the increasing power of feminism as a
worldwide movement for revisioning and reforming human
reality derives from the fact that it is a comprehensive ideology in both the theoretical and the practical senses of the
word. It draws its initiating energy from the actual experience of oppression which consciousness raising enables
women to recognize and appropriate. It engages in a focused
social analysis which has revealed the role of patriarchy not
only as the root of women's oppression but also as the source
of the interconnectedness of sexism with all other forms of
hierarchical domination, thus relating women's liberation
to the universal movement toward liberation abroad in the
world. It offers a comprehensive vision of an alternative future and has undertaken a multi-pronged program to bring

that future into being. Because women are not a particular social class or subgroup but at least half of virtually every natural grouping and social class in the world and because the process of consciousness-raising is universally accessible, at least in principle, there is good reason to believe, as some have suggested, that the women's movement is the most powerful movement in the history of the world and that history cannot continue unchanged in the face of this rising of half the race.

IV. Feminism and the Church

Feminism began as a secular movement, but within a few years of the rise of the "second wave" in the 1960s feminists began to see the profound connection between patriarchy and organized religion. Although feminism has brought its critique to bear on virtually all of the world's religions, for the sake of clarity and focus I will restrict my considerations to Christianity in general, and Catholicism in particular. Most Catholic feminists would probably agree in dating the beginning of the Catholic feminist movement to 1968 when Mary Daly published her manifesto, *The Church and the Second Sex.*[39] There is no question that Daly saw, before most Catholic feminists did, that the Catholic Church was a major participant in the oppression of women and that this was not an accidental historical development but a major systemic problem with Catholicism itself. In 1971, in Harvard Memorial Church, Daly called Christian women to realize that there was no place for them in the church as it understands itself. She ended her proclamation with an invitation to the women present to walk, as an exodus community, out of the church, the land of our fathers, and into the future of true sisterhood.[40] Not only did the women present that day follow Daly out of the church building, but many have followed her out of Catholicism and into alternate forms of feminist spirituality, a topic to which we will return.

The Catholic feminist analysis began[41] in ecclesial consciousness-raising, i.e. in the realization by many Catholic women that they were excluded from significant dimensions of the Catholic experience. They were totally excluded from one of the seven sacraments, holy orders, and consequently from all real participation in leadership and decision-making in the church, and were told that this exclusion was based on the divine will regarding the female of the species and was therefore theologically based and irreformable. Furthermore, even in those areas in which they were allowed to participate, for example in the liturgical assembly, they were effectively rendered invisible by being linguistically subsumed into all-male categories as "men," "brothers," and "sons" and denied the right to exercise even non-ordained functions that were open to male children, such as reading as lectors or serving at the altar as acolytes. At the same time, women were rendered totally dependent upon men for access to the sacraments of daily life. Some women even pointed to the close parallel in psychological experience between physical rape and the forced spiritual stripping of women's consciences, particularly in the sexual sphere, before male judges in the confessional.

Not only were women excluded, marginalized, and degraded in the church, but they were also directly oppressed by church authorities, and the church legitimated and supported their oppression by men in family and society. Women religious realized that they could not exercise even minimal self-determination within their own congregations while married women had no leverage whatever in the decisions made by male celibates about even the most intimate details of their lives as wives and mothers. The church's pastoral practice discouraged women from seeking divorce from abusive husbands, forbade the divorced to remarry under any circumstances, counseled them to accept spouse abuse as God's will, commanded them to yield to marital rape, and forbade them to use contraceptives to control the results of such abuse or to have recourse to abortion in cases of rape or incest.

In short, the church was a prime legitimator of patriarchal marriage and its attendant abuses. By its romantic reduction of women's identity and role to motherhood and its definition of the family in patriarchal terms of male headship, church authorities constricted women's self-image, loaded women's emergence into the public sphere with guilt, and legitimated patriarchal structures of economic discrimination designed to keep women out of the work force and dependent on the male head of the household.

At the same time that the church excluded women from full participation in the sacramental system and from any participation in church leadership, legitimated their oppression in the family, and collaborated in their societal marginalization, the church used women for virtually all ecclesiastical tasks that men did not care to perform while underpaying them, denying them all access to power, and leaving them totally dependent on the good will and tolerance of male power figures. Women ministered by the permission of men, on male terms, only in those spheres permitted to them by men, for whatever pay men decided to give them, and subject to whatever employment conditions and/or dismissal procedures men chose to impose.

As Catholic women's consciousness was raised about their experience in the church they began to realize that their exclusion, marginalization, and oppression were not incidental or accidental but structural and systemic. They identified the church as a deeply patriarchal structure, owned and operated by men for their own benefit, and firmly committed to the continued domination of women Catholics by men in general and male clerics in particular.

This social analysis of the church led directly to the basic theological question: Is the church patriarchal by merely human or by divine dispensation? In other words, did God in Christ ordain women's secondary and subordinate position in Christianity, or have male hierarchs distorted the Christian message in their own patriarchal image? If the former hypothesis is the case, then women can only remain Catholics at the price of their self-respect as humans and believers.[42] If, however, the church's patriarchal structure and function is a distortion of the gospel, then Catholic feminists have an enormous and exhausting task on their hands, viz. the radical transformation of the church,[43] but it makes sense for those who can endure the pain to remain and to struggle until the church becomes the "discipleship of equals"[44] which Jesus initiated.[45]

This basic question about the divine or human origin of the church's patriarchal character has been engaged from within every theological discipline. Systematic theologians have undertaken a radical rereading of the dogmatic tradition.[46] Ecclesiologists have raised specific questions about the constitution of the church and its original ministerial structure; moral theologians about women as subjects of conscience and about the definition of female sexuality against a presumed male norm; church historians about the lost and/or distorted story of women in the development of the church; pastoral theologians about the results of the exclusion of women's gifts from the church's ministerial experience.

At the basis of these questions, however, are two fundamental issues upon which the continued participation of women in the Christian tradition finally depends. First, is the God of Judaeo-Christian revelation a male being who sent a divine male to save us, thus revealing the normativity of maleness and establishing the superiority of males in relation to females in the order of salvation? Second, did God create one human nature in which women and men participate fully and equally, or is human nature dual with men called by nature to full participation in the Christian mystery in the image of God and the likeness of Christ and women called to a derivative identity and role in the likeness of men? In short, the ultimate questions are theological and anthropological. What is the true nature of God and what is the true nature of humanity? Do the answers to these questions support male supremacy as divinely ordained or do they allow for the genuine equality of man and woman in the divine plan?

The need to answer these questions brings us finally to the issue of the interpretation of scripture. If the Bible is the ultimate norm against which Christian faith and practice must be measured, we cannot escape the question of what the scriptures say about the nature of God and human nature. What started as a substantive question about the doctrinal content of scripture rapidly progressed toward more subtle questions about the imagery and symbolism for God in the Bible, the gendered quality of language about God and about humans in scripture, the pervasive androcentrism of sacred history, and finally about the very process and meaning of biblical interpretation itself.

V. Conclusion

In the preceding paragraphs I have attempted to clarify the fundamental terminology of feminism, to supply a relatively complete descriptive definition of the contemporary feminist movement at least as it is developing among white, western, middle-class feminists in the first world,[47] and to sketch the basic contours of the engagement between feminist consciousness and the Catholic experience. If my description and analyses are at all true to the historical phenomenon, the answer to the question posed in the title of this essay should be clear. Feminism is not a fad or the passing obsession of a few disgruntled women. Feminism is a worldwide movement that envisions nothing less than the radical transformation of human history. It maintains that such a transformation is necessary in order for over half of the human race to be able to participate fully in the human enterprise. But it also maintains that until women participate in that enterprise, the human family and the earth as its home remain in mortal danger. Women do not seek to participate as imitation males or on male terms in a male construction of reality. Rather they have undertaken a deconstruction of male reality and a reconstruction of reality in more human terms. If the feminist enterprise succeeds, the future of humanity will be qualitatively different. I have been trying to suggest that the change will be in the direction of salvation for the race and for the planet.

2

Scripture: Tool of Patriarchy or Resource for Transformation?

I. Introduction

If feminism is a major resource for the transformation of humanity and history in the direction of wholeness and hope, it is also a serious challenge to organized religion and especially to Christianity because it calls into question the traditional theology of God and of human beings. But beneath these theological questions lies an even more fundamental issue, namely the question of biblical revelation. The question, in its starkest terms, is whether or not the Bible teaches the maleness of God and the inferiority of women. In other words, is patriarchy divinely revealed and therefore divinely sanctioned? It would seem that, if it is, there is no future for self-affirming women in Christianity because the Bible is regarded by Christians as somehow a bearer of divine revelation.

The uniquely privileged place that the Bible holds in Christian faith is expressed in various ways in different Christian communions but, in effect, all agree that it is the touchstone of the faith. Vatican II in the dogmatic constitution on divine revelation, *Dei Verbum,* called scripture, which the church venerates "as she venerate[s] the Body of the Lord" in the eucharist, "the pure and perennial source" of the spiritual life (VI, 21).[1] Authentic Christian faith cannot bypass scripture. But a God who reveals women's intrinsic inferiority cannot function salvifically for women. Indeed, such a God cannot finally function salvifically for men either because this God would be the legitimator of men's oppression of women and, in the last analysis, oppression is destructive of the oppressor as well as of the victim.

As feminist biblical scholarship has progressed during the past two decades it has become virtually impossible to pretend that the long established tradition of invoking biblical authority to justify the oppression of women in family, society, and church is based solely on a misreading of scripture. Without doubt there have been misogynist misinterpretations of scripture in the course of history, but it is no longer possible to deny that the text itself is not only androcentric, i.e. a male-centered account of male experience for male purposes with women relegated to the margins of salvation history, but also patriarchal in its assumptions and often in its explicit teaching, and at times deeply sexist, i.e. antiwoman. Its God-language and imagery are overwhelmingly male. When the official church invokes scripture to justify its discriminatory treatment of women it does not have to resort to fundamentalist prooftexting or to questionable exegetical methods. In other words, the problem is in the text.

Some women, of course, have accepted and interiorized what seems to be the biblical verdict on their status, namely that male headship in family and church is divinely mandated, that women's subordination is of divine institution, and that God is ultimately, if not actually male, at least the warrant for regarding the male as the normative human being. In biblical fundamentalist communities there is virtually no alternative to accepting these conclusions and their practical implications.

Other women, whose number is increasing, have examined the biblical material and, having found overwhelming evidence of its androcentric, patriarchal, and sexist character, have concluded that the biblical text is so totally and irredeemably oppressive of women, so destructive of female personhood, that it cannot possibly proclaim the true God or function as word of God for self-respecting women. Those with the courage of their convictions have severed their ties with institutional Christianity and taken their religious quest elsewhere. We will return to this subject in the next chapter.

Finally, there are some women who have neither agreed to a seemingly biblically mandated inferiority nor found a way to avoid the problematic conclusions of sound exegesis. And yet, leaving Christianity behind is not a viable option for them. These are women who recognize not only the damage that Christianity has inflicted on women but also its positive effects. Furthermore, they also realize that western culture is thoroughly imbued with biblical influence. One cannot simply walk away from Christianity because its values and presuppositions color all of our western institutions, social processes, and relational patterns. One does not have to be a registered Christian to feel the effects of biblical misogynism and leaving institutional Christianity will not protect one from them. But even more importantly these women have deep personal reasons for wanting to remain Christian. Their spirituality is profoundly christocentric and the roots of their identity and personal history are deep in the soil of Christianity. It is these women who have continued to struggle with the question, both theological and exegetical, of the Bible and its role in Christian faith.

If we agree that the question is simply "What does the

Bible say about women?" and that the sole method for answering that question is historical critical exegesis, our
options are severely limited. I want to suggest that this for-
mulation of the question does not go deep enough and that
exegesis is an insufficient approach to the answer. The first
question that must be asked is what we mean by the basic
faith assertion that the Bible is the word of God. Then exegesis must be subsumed into a larger project of interpretation
in order to discover not just "what the Bible says" but what
the scriptures, as word of God, mean for the Christian community today.

In approaching these questions two extremes are to be
disavowed at the outset. The first is extreme biblical liberalism according to which the Bible is merely a "book like any
other book," one written in a time and culture whose presuppositions about such things as miracles, cosmology, or divine
speech, and therefore perhaps also about the nature and
status of women, are no longer credible and therefore do not
have to be either accepted or refuted but merely exposed
and explained. The extreme biblical liberal does not share
the problem of the believing feminist for whom the Bible
remains authoritative, because for the extreme liberal "word
of God" is simply a reverential designation for a book which,
however dear to Christians, is no more nor less authoritative
than its content, judged by current norms of rationality,
warrants.

The second extreme position is that of the biblical fundamentalist for whom the Bible is literally the word of God.
Although fundamentalists cover a broad spectrum the position itself involves three presuppositions which, in my opinion, are false in themselves but which, more importantly for
our purposes here, foreclose any attempt to deal with the
morally problematic aspects of scripture in a liberating way.[2]

First, fundamentalism rests on the faulty theological presupposition of verbal inspiration, a presupposition which founders on the results of modern biblical criticism such as multiple authorship of some books of the Bible, historical processes of composition which sometimes spanned centuries, and clear historical and scientific errors of fact in the text.

Second, it rests on the erroneous literary presupposition that there is such a thing as "face value" in literary texts; that one can read a text without interpreting it and that this is, indeed, the best and only honest way to read it. In fact, the only way we can understand texts is by interpreting them, and the richer, more complicated, and distant from us by language and culture the text is, the more necessary and complex will be the required process of interpretation. The question is not whether we will interpret the text, but how.[3] The refusal to interpret is a particular kind of interpretation and one which is not justified by our human experience with texts and reading.

Third, fundamentalism rests on a faulty spiritual presupposition which involves a quasi-magical view of the biblical text. Magic is the attempt to influence, even control, divine action by use of certain techniques. The fundamentalist approach to scripture attempts to make God respond to a disordered human need for absolute certitude. Christian faith affirms that, as Vatican II said, God comes to meet us in and through the scriptures,[4] but this divine encounter does not involve a divine promise to answer our felt needs for absolute authority in our lives which is really a deep desire to escape the human condition.

For reasons very different from those of the extreme liberal, the biblical fundamentalist is also unlikely to struggle with the question with which we are dealing. However, people who are not fundamentalists in the doctrinal or confessional sense are often naive literalists in their approach to scripture. For a literalist the processes of exegesis are respected but, once the so-called "literal sense" of a text has been established, the interpretative enterprise is closed. Like the fundamentalist, the literalist stops with the answer to the question "What does the text say?" which is thought to be equivalent to what the author meant and/or how the text was understood in the historical setting to which it was first addressed. As we have already noted, the answer to that question often cannot be other than damaging for women.

II. Meaning of the Affirmation: Scripture Is the Word of God

Christians of all varieties are united in affirming that, in some sense of the term, scripture is the word of God. This affirmation usually goes unexamined and, as has been said, can signify anything from religious reverence for the book itself to an extreme fundamentalistic belief that every word of scripture was literally dictated by God to a human scribe who wrote it down without error. Most Christians are somewhere between these two extremes but are hard put to say exactly what calling scripture the word of God signifies theologically. I propose to break the question down into two parts. First, what kind of linguistic entity is the term "word of God"? Second, to what does the term refer?

A. *The Linguistic Expression: A Metaphor*

To inquire into the linguistic nature of the term "word of God" is to ask what kind of language we are using when we use this term. At the very least we must admit that the term cannot be a literal designation of the Bible. To call scripture the word of God is to attribute intelligible discourse to God. But God does not think discursively and does not speak in words.

Discursive thought is the sequential mental process of limited beings whose rationality does not and cannot involve immediate and complete spiritual coincidence with the known. Furthermore, words are physical sounds (or their visible representatives), produced by vocal cords, as expressions of human rational and affective processes of some kind. Such speech is both our most powerful method of self-expression and an ultimately limited and inadequate method. The limitations of speech itself are evident in the impossibility of perfectly translating speech from one language to another. Without words we can say nothing at all, but our words can never express perfectly the self we strive to bring to disclosure by speech. In short, speech is a radically human experience, rooted in our bodiliness and expressive of our sequential thought processes, and therefore essentially and not just accidentally finite. Nothing in this descriptive definition of speech can be literally predicated of God who is pure spirit and therefore literally neither thinks nor speaks.

To deny that scripture is literally the "word of God" because God does not literally speak is not necessarily to claim that the expression is ultimately meaningless or radically untrue. It is to realize that "word of God" is, strictly speaking, a metaphor. A metaphor is not simply an abbreviated simile whose tenor can be translated into literal language once its meaning is understood, or a mere rhetorical decoration that makes discourse more interesting or effective. Metaphor is our most effective access to meaning which cannot be expressed literally because it transcends in some way the ostensible reality of everyday experience.

A metaphor is recognizable by the fact that, at the literal level, it is absurd and yet it carries meaning. It is not false, as is, e.g. the erroneous statement, "Cats are canines." The metaphor conveys meaning but in such a way that the mind must reach beyond, without negating the relevance of, the literal expression.[5] The metaphor suggests the direction of meaning but does not simply deliver it. It invites the whole psyche—intelligence, feeling, imagination—into play in search of meaning which is indicated but not delivered. "Hungrily his eyes searched hers" conveys meaning. But taken literally it would be absurd. Eyes cannot literally hunger or search, nor can they be searched.

A metaphor is a predication which involves an unresolved tension between an "is" and an "is not," an affirmation and a negation, predicated of the same thing at the same time. At the literal level what is affirmed must be denied, i.e. it "is not." But at some other level, some deeper and more important level, the affirmation is true. This is the "is." To say that "Individualism is the cancer of our society" is to speak metaphorically. At the literal level individualism "is not" a physical disease which can be treated by surgery or chemotherapy. But the metaphorical statement evokes not just an intellectual grasp of the life-gone-wild character of rampant individualism but also the emotional response of fear, revulsion, hopelessness in the face of a silently spreading malignancy, and a desperate sense of urgency. It also evokes an organismic understanding of society with all the philosophical and sociological freight that this foundational metaphor carries. If we agree with the negative judgment on individualism carried by this metaphor it conveys more truth than a literal analysis of the phenomenon does. But whether or not we agree with it, the metaphor is more powerful in its appeal to the whole psyche than a non-metaphorical, i.e. a literal, description of individualism.

Because the metaphor lives in the tension between the "is not" of the literal level and the "is" at the evocative level, a metaphor is a very unstable linguistic entity. There is a constant and inveterate tendency of the mind to resolve the tension by choosing between the "is" and the "is not." If one suppresses the "is" one destroys the metaphor by simply denying its applicability to the subject matter. Thus, one says that society is not literally an organism and individualism is not literally a physical disease and consequently there is nothing to worry about.

If one suppresses the "is not" one literalizes the metaphor. A literalized metaphor has been killed, but not all dead metaphors are buried. Most metaphors eventually die and they are buried in the semantic field of the language. For example, "leg" was originally a metaphorical way of speaking of that which holds up a table. Now, one of the dictionary meanings of the word "leg" is "part of a piece of furniture." The metaphor has been literalized and interred in the language.

However, some metaphors refer to realities which are both unavailable to ordinary experience and tremendously significant for personal or social experience. Therefore, when such metaphors are literalized, it often is not noticed because there is nothing in our sensible experience against which to check the affirmation. These are the dead but unburied metaphors which pollute their imaginative environment distorting both cognition and affectivity. Such a dead metaphor, at least in the imagination of most Christians, is "God is our Father." For such believers God is, for all intents and purposes, literally a male being who rules over his patriarchal household, the human family, as earthly fathers rule over theirs. For such people, it is no more appropriate to call this heavenly father "mother" than to call our human fathers "mother." And all non-human metaphors for God are reduced to similes because their "is" cannot be taken seriously in regard to a God who is literally a male person, a father.

Finally, there are metaphors which never die, whose tensiveness is ultimately unresolvable because their tenor is so intrinsically irreducible to their vehicle that the mental equation necessary for their literalization cannot be carried out. For example, the metaphor of the church as body of Christ is difficult to literalize because the church is so evidently not a physical body that the "is not" cannot be suppressed. Such resistant metaphors have a pronounced capacity to function as "root metaphors,"[6] i.e. metaphors which draw semantic nourishment from a wide range of experience, while they generate, support, and organize a rich growth of imaginative fruit in the form of dependent and related metaphors. Sallie McFague has suggested that the root metaphor of Christianity is "reign of God,"[7] an eschatological reality which not only focuses hope but names whatever has been achieved which is recognizable as that hope in process of realization.

What kind of metaphor is the expression "word of God"? Although it is susceptible to both destruction and literalization, I would propose that it is best understood as a root metaphor because, as soon as one reflects deeply on the metaphor, its metaphorical quality "revives." One can, of course, like the extreme liberal, deny the "is" and treat "word of God" as a reverential designation of a book which is not, in any real sense of the word, divine. And one can, like the fundamentalist, suppress the "is not" and treat the Bible as literally God's speech. But the first position runs counter to the profound faith conviction of the Christian community that there is something special, unique, even divine about the Bible. The second position runs counter to the results of the best biblical scholarship and, increasingly, to the common sense of ordinary believers. Both faith and reason conspire to identify the proposition "The Bible is the word of God" as a metaphor. It evokes felt meaning but it does not deliver literal sense.

This metaphor is not, however, an ordinary one. It is a root metaphor because its nourishing ground is the entire tradition of biblical revelation and because its fruit is a rich and diversified range of interaction between God and humans in the sphere of interpersonal self-communication.

B. *Referent of "Word of God": Symbolic Revelation*

If word of God is a metaphor, its function is to convey meaning which exceeds our capacities for literal expression, which is too rich to be captured by literal speech, but which is neither unintelligible nor unavailable. We must, then, inquire after its referent, that to which it points. I suggest that the referent of the metaphor word of God is symbolic divine revelation.

Revelation is not the imparting of secret information, even though it does have a noetic dimension. Revelation is, first and foremost, self-gift, the communication or sharing of one's subjectivity. One's self is the ultimately unavailable. Virtually any other kind of knowledge is, in principle, available to any qualified researcher. But the "knowing" involved in personal relationship is different precisely because we cannot come to know another unless the other invites us into that intimacy, makes it possible for us through the self-gift of revelation.

Language plays a singularly important role in the process of self-revelation. Far from being primarily a system of labels which we affix to discreet entities of experience, language is first of all the activity in and through which we bring our selves to disclosure, make ourselves intersubjectively available. Language is intrinsically symbolic because it is the extension of body which is the primary symbol in human experience. Unlike a sign which stands for something other than itself, as an exit sign stands for a doorway or a red light stands for the command to stop, a symbol is a way of being present to something which cannot be present in any other way. Our body, and its extensions in language, both spoken and gestural, is our way of being present. It is the symbol of our person which cannot be present in intersubjective availability except through symbolic self-expression.

Symbolic expression is both the only way personal subjectivity can render itself present and always necessarily an inadequate and ambiguous rendering. The symbolic expression never exhausts the reality being expressed, thus necessitating endless reexpression as the speaker struggles to disclose the fullness of her or his thought or feeling. But no matter how adequate the expression it never coincides totally with what is being expressed, and thus it remains ambiguous, capable of being misunderstood. Consequently, symbolic expression only functions in interaction with interpretation, and no interpretation is fully adequate, complete, exhaustive. While this seems, at first sight, to be a tragedy rendering communication always imperfect and often false, it is also the source of the endless and ever new interaction which is the special delight of friends and lovers. The person who invites us into intimacy through symbolic self-revelation can never be definitively known but remains a reservoir of meaning drawing us ever onward and inward in the quest for personal communion in the mystery of being.

However divine revelation is understood, it is first and foremost not an extraterrestrial source of accurate information but God's self-gift to humans. Christians believe that God invites human beings to be "partakers of the divine nature" (2 Pet 1:4), to enter into the divine life of God which is opened to us through divine revelation. That revelation is necessarily symbolic, i.e. suited to our mode of intersubjective knowing. But because it is symbolic it is always limited, inadequate to its infinite subject, ambiguous and therefore in need of endless interpretation. The infinity of divine subjectivity requires but is never exhausted by symbolic revelation.

Divine self-revelation is actually coextensive with reality because whatever exists speaks of its creator, of the source of its being. However, Christian reflection has identified three primary spheres of revelation: nature, history, and humanity. The psalms especially speak of the glory of God revealed in the wonders of nature where day speaks to day of God's beauty and night pours out knowledge (cf. Ps 19:1–3), where the voice of God thunders in the cataracts (cf. Ps 42:7), and the power of God is unleashed in storm and earthquake (cf. Ps 18:7–15). The Hebrews were not the only peoples to discern the presence and action of God in the mighty displays of nature as well as in her beneficence to all living things. The special insight of the Hebrews was their realization that God also acted in history, revealing God's nature and designs for all people but especially for those whom God had chosen by bringing them out of captivity, establishing them in their own land, and giving them a law incorporating the divine Wisdom as no other law before had ever done (cf. Wis 10–11).

Ultimately, however, God resorted to human language, speaking through specially chosen messengers, the prophets of the Old Testament and eventually Jesus of Nazareth. Just as nature can be regarded as God's self-manifestation and history can be understood as the experience of God's interaction with the people, so the oracles of the prophets can be regarded as God's speech. But nature remains nature, history remains history, and humans remain humans even as they serve as symbolic material for divine self-communication. They do not cease to be limited, imperfect, ambiguous, in need of endless interpretation if they are to function as God's symbolic self-expression.

The real referent of the expression "word of God" is divine symbolic self-revelation. The choice of the term "word" is both appropriate and dangerous; appropriate because language is our most adequate mode of symbolic self-revelation and dangerous because it is too easy for us to imagine God as a person in our image speaking as we speak. This danger is compounded when the term is applied not to nature or history or prophetic spokespersons but to the Bible which is indeed a verbal reality, a document written in words.

For Christians the ultimate divine self-revelation is not the Bible but Jesus, the word of God incarnate. But the temptation to see scripture, precisely because it is a linguistic reality, as the ultimate divine self-revelation is powerful. It is a temptation that must be resisted if a nuanced and theologically accurate understanding of scripture is to be developed. Such an understanding is the only basis for a theory of interpretation which can both take seriously the unique role of the Bible in Christian faith and respond to the challenge raised by the very real limitations of the biblical text. Symbolic revelation is the locus of encounter with God but it is, like all symbolic communication, only capable of mediating such an encounter through the never exhaustive process of human interpretation because all symbols are inherently and invincibly ambiguous, simultaneously revealing and concealing as they lead us into interpersonal intimacy.

III. Relation of the Bible to Divine Revelation

If word of God is a metaphor for the full range of symbolic divine revelation in nature, history, prophecy, human beings and especially Jesus, we must raise the question of what role scripture plays in this multi-faceted interaction between God and humanity. In other words, we must ask "What is the relationship between scripture and revelation?"

First, it should be evident that scripture is not identical with revelation. Revelation cannot be reduced to the Bible for it is a much more inclusive term. Second, the Bible is not the paradigmatic instance of revelation, a role that Christians assign only to Jesus. Third, the Bible does not contain revelation the way a dictionary contains definitions or a newspaper contains stock market information. Revelation is not primarily information and its primary form is not propositions. The linguistic text has some relationship to revelation but the nature of that relationship is more complex and subtle than the relationship of a container to its contents.

Perhaps the best category for understanding the relationship of text to revelation is witness. The Bible bears witness to that special revelation which Christians believe occurred in the history of Israel and the early church and especially in the life, death, and resurrection of Jesus of Nazareth. Witness is always in some way a language event, a verbal or quasi-verbal testimony to one's experience and therefore to that which has been experienced. However, no matter how faithful the witness it never delivers the reality of the event as such. Witness is always at least two removes from the reality in question. The first remove is the interpreting experience of the person who is the witness. The second remove is the recounting of the interpreting experience in the giving of testimony.

Because testimony or witness always involves the interpretation of the event by the witness and then the verbal shaping of the event in the testimony itself, no witness is ever fully adequate to its subject matter. Furthermore, as human testimony it is virtually always biased in some way by its position within the horizon of a particular witness. At times testimony which is essentially true can even involve errors of fact or interpretation. For example, I can give true witness to the fact that car A ran a stop sign and collided with car B which was proceeding legally even though I may be in error about the color of the cars or the name of the street where they collided. Of course, the more errors of fact my testimony involves, the less credibility is likely to be assigned to my witness. And some errors would render the witness useless.

Because of the necessarily limited, biased, and error-prone character of all human testimony precisely because it involves interpretation by the witness and because it must be set forth in the available linguistic genres, the receiving of witness is itself an essentially hermeneutical enterprise. All testimony must be interpreted. This involves not only ascertaining the competence and honesty of the witness but also interrogating the testimony given. Once we have identified scripture as a case of human verbal witness to divine revelation we must accept the consequences, namely, that we must not only ascertain the competence of the witnesses but also examine the testimony for the shortcomings and inadequacies that are part of all human witness and then interpret the testimony using all the skills available to us.

Word of God, then, is a metaphor for the totality of divine revelation, especially as it is expressed in Jesus. The Bible is a witness to the human experience of divine revelation. In other words, it is a limited, biased, human testimony to a limited experience of God's self-gift. The Bible is not divine revelation nor does it contain divine revelation. It contains the necessarily inadequate, sometimes even erroneous, verbal expression of the experience of divine revelation of those who were privileged subjects of that gift of God. In other words, it is not God who is limited but the modes through which we can experience God and the modes by which we can express that experience. The Bible is literally the word of human beings about their experience of God. Metaphorically it can be called the word of God because of the subject matter of that human discourse and the power of the experience which comes to expression in it. But it is not thereby made literally divine speech nor is it invested with the inerrancy of divinity.

The foregoing reflection brings us back to our original dilemma, the morally unacceptable content of scripture. Although our concern is with the biblical material which is harmful to the personhood of women, it must be recalled that the Bible also contains racist and anti-semitic material as well as morally objectionable attitudes toward war attributed directly to God. In other words, the problem raised by feminists is not limited to women. The large question is how a text which has been found morally wanting in some respects can function normatively for a community called to justice and liberation.

One approach to the objectionable material, and one which is generally regarded as unacceptable, is to excise the offending material if not physically at least by silencing it in the community. A second approach which is useful but, in my opinion, still not adequate is the purely exegetical. Feminist scholars have devoted considerable effort to the important task of exegeting from a feminist perspective the texts of Old and New Testament which deal directly with women in an effort to highlight the occasional positive presentations of women and their role in salvation history[8] as well as the liberating praxis of Jesus in regard to women.[9]

Other scholars have turned to the exegesis of blatantly sexist texts such as the "tales of terror" in the Old Testament,[10] or such New Testament texts as 1 Cor 11:3–16; 14:34–36; Col 3:18–19; Eph 5:22–33; 1 Tim 2:8–15; Tit 2:4–5; and 1 Pet 3:1–7,[11] in order to make visible what has been silenced in the history of God's people as well as to demonstrate the occasional character and culturally limited valence of such texts.

More ambitious projects of an historical nature have been undertaken by scholars such as Elisabeth Schüssler Fiorenza in *In Memory of Her*. In this master work Fiorenza interrogates the entire New Testament in order to force it to yield the suppressed history of women in early Christianity and, by restoring women to Christian history, restore their history to Christian women.

All of these efforts are necessary and helpful. But they do not address the fundamental question of how an intrinsically oppressive text, one which is actually morally offensive in some respects, can function normatively in and for the believing community. In what sense can one regard as word of God that which, in some respects at least, cannot possibly be attributed to God without rendering God the enemy and oppressor of some human beings?

IV. Beyond Exegesis to Hermeneutics

The approach I want to take to this question goes beyond exegesis into the realm of philosophy, a philosophy of written discourse and a philosophy of interpretation, in order to arrive finally at a theology of interpretation. At the outset I want to set aside definitively any appeal to the special religious character of scripture as a solution to the problem since that is precisely what is called into question by the morally objectionable material in the Bible. In other words, I do not want to claim that scripture must be finally and somehow salvific because it is divinely inspired. Whatever may be said about a "fuller sense" of scripture or the progressive nature of revelation in salvation history is outside the realm of the present inquiry precisely because both of these approaches involve claims that cannot be investigated without appeal to the faith which is threatened by the very text under scrutiny. It is the biblical basis itself of faith that requires investigation.

I propose to examine the nature of the biblical text *as text,* i.e. as a human literary construct purporting to bear witness to the experience of divine revelation, and interpretation *as a human enterprise,* i.e. as a work of human understanding. I am asking whether there is a way to understand text and interpretation which allows us to acknowledge honestly what we cannot deny, namely the moral problems inherent in the text, and to continue to claim this text as normative and liberating for the Christian community.

A. *The Nature of a Text*

Within the contemporary community of biblical scholars there are basically two understandings of texts. The first, which admits of much variety that runs the gamut from rank fundamentalism to very nuanced historical criticism, is an essentially positivist position. The text is regarded as a kind of semantic container, separate from and independent of the reader, and permanently circumscribed by the conditions and circumstances of its production. Its meaning, which was determined by its author, was put into the text by the act of writing, and it remains constant throughout the history of its interpretation even though readers may be able to understand that meaning more or less adequately at different times.

Exegesis is the process through which, by the correct application of appropriate methods, one extracts from the text the meaning intended and established by the author. In short, a text means what its author intended it to mean, and the task of the exegete is to discover what that meaning is. This semantic content of the text is known as its "literal sense." Once literal sense has been ascertained to the best of the ability of the exegete, it can be taken up by theologians and pastors who, by allowing it to interact with the tradition and experience of the believing community, apply it to contemporary situations in a theologically, religiously, or spiritually relevant way. The process of exegesis, however, is independent of later applications. Not all applications are equally valid, and their degree of validity must be judged according to their fidelity to the literal sense.

In the course of church history the positivist approach to the text has supported three basic modes of handling the increasing historical gap between the literal sense and the contemporary context. The typically Protestant approach involves a more or less complete surrender to the text. The typically Catholic approach involves submitting the text to ecclesiastical authority which supplements (and sometimes supplants or suppresses) its meaning by recourse to "tradition." Finally, the biblical fideist manages to live relatively comfortably in two worlds, affirming intellectually the historical literal sense of the text while adhering in faith to what the church teaches and believes even if it is neither contained in nor supported by the text. In every case exegesis is the limit of the positivist approach to the text.

The second understanding of text, one which is gaining increasing acceptance among biblical scholars and which is the one upon which I will draw in what follows, is essentially linguistic and literary rather than purely historical. It regards the text not as a semantic container but as a structured mediation of meaning. Meaning is not contained in the text; it is an event of understanding which takes place in the encounter between text and reader. The text, then, is never fully independent of the reader except in the most banal and physicalist sense of the word.

Like a musical score, which is not really music but only the normative possibility of music awaiting actualization by the one who plays it, the text does not contain meaning but provides a normative possibility for making meaning which can be realized by a competent reader. Because every reader is different the interaction of text and reader will never be exactly the same twice. However, just as not all interpre-

tations of a musical score are equally good, not all interpretations of a text are equally good; indeed not all interpretations
are valid. Thus, it is necessary to develop criteria of validity
and to submit diverse interpretations to these criteria applied both by the community of scholars and by the community of believers.[12] The text norms the interpretation, but
no interpretation is *the* one and only correct one, and the
interpretative enterprise will never terminate in a final and
uniquely valid interpretation. Such a final interpretation is
not only not possible; it is not even desirable.

For those who regard a text this way, exegesis is a moment in a larger process of interpretation. The quest for
meaning does not terminate in the intention of the author,
and the distance between ancient text and contemporary
interpreter must be bridged in and by the interpretation
itself, not by means of a separate and subsequent process of
theological or homiletic application. Interpretation termin-
ates in the transformation of the reader whose horizon of
self-understanding now coincides, at least to some degree,
with the horizon of the world of the text. The reader begins
to live "in a different world" which involves being somehow
a different person. This transformation can be either positive
or negative. Our question is whether a woman who enters
into this process of interpretation must necessarily emerge
into a world that constricts and debases her or whether the
text can mediate a self-transcending transformation toward
liberation.

B. *The Process of Interpretation*

Hans-Georg Gadamer proposed the fruitful analogy of
legal hermeneutics[13] which has been exploited by subsequent theorists to illuminate the question of how ancient
classical texts can be made to function normatively in subse-

quent historical situations. The judge faces incessantly the problem of how to apply a law formulated in the past to a case in the present which is often radically different because of the changed historical situation.

Linnell Cady, in a recent article, proposed a typology of juridical approaches to this dilemma.[14] In the first approach the judge considers himself or herself absolutely constrained by precedent, i.e. by the way in which the law has been applied in the past. If precedent exists the judge has no choice but to follow it. Only in cases where there is no precedent can the judge improvise, thereby creating a precedent which will be binding for subsequent judgments. The problem with this approach is that, as social experience becomes more complex, the law appears more primitive and unadapted to the cases to which it is being applied until such time as it becomes completely useless and must be rescinded and/or replaced.

In the second approach, at the other extreme, the judge considers himself or herself completely unrestrained by precedent. Here the judge interprets the law according to current understandings of goodness and justice, without appeal to the mediation of precedent. The problem here is that there is no continuity between current jurisprudence and the community's historical experience. The community is adrift in the sea of contemporary wisdom guided only by maps which become ever more out of date as time passes because they have not been updated through a process of consistent interpretation.

The third approach is one in which the judge is constrained by precedent but not absolutely constrained. The judge does not ignore precedent but interprets precedent in the light of the community's ongoing experience, including its current understandings of justice. The question, of course, is how the judge arrives at that vision of the whole which enables him or her to read the law, mediated by precedent, through the lens of current perceptions of justice and thus apply it to the case before the court. This is precisely the question faced by the biblical interpreter, the challenge of being simultaneously faithful on the one hand to the text and the tradition of interpretation and on the other to contemporary perceptions of justice and liberation so that the text can be allowed to function normatively but not oppressively in the faith community.

1. Conditions of Possibility for an Actualizing Hermeneutics

The work of the philosopher Paul Ricoeur on the nature of the written text is very useful for our purposes.[15] Ricoeur challenged the unreflective assumption that a text is simply "talk writ down," i.e. that writing is just a fixed form of oral discourse. He pointed out several essential differences between oral and written discourse which bear directly on the process of interpreting texts.

First, what does *not* happen when a text is composed is that its meaning becomes fixed in such wise that the text means forever whatever the author meant when he or she wrote it. Furthermore, contrary to what Plato and his successors taught,[16] the writing of a text does not render the vivid meaning of the oral discourse fainter, necessitating an effort to "revive" the meaning whose faint traces are found in the text. Texts, said Ricoeur, are not oral discourse committed to paper but a different kind of discourse altogether.

When discourse is committed to writing, three effects occur. First, the meaning of the text is sheltered from destruction. It is no longer dependent upon the memory of those who heard it but can survive not only the disappearance of the author but even that of the original audience.

Second, inscription invests the text with what Ricoeur

calls "semantic autonomy." The meaning of the text is cut loose from the author's intention. As long as the speaker is speaking, the hearers can question what they do not understand and the speaker can correct the hearers' interpretations. The discourse remains under the control of the speaker and it means really and only what the speaker intends, whether or not the hearers understand it. But once the discourse has been written down, "[w]hat the text signifies no longer coincides with what the author meant; henceforth, textual meaning and psychological meaning have different destinies."[17] The text now means whatever it can mean and all that it can mean. Meaning is no longer limited to authorial intention but is mediated by the structures of the text. Students often learn this painfully when their grade reflects what their test paper actually says and not what they meant or intended to say. Thus, a text might mean much more (or much less!) than its author actually understood or intended. The "much more" is what has been called the "surplus of meaning" in so-called classical texts.[18] The semantic autonomy of a text is not absolute because meaning continues to be mediated by the structures of the text which remain constant through multiple and diverse interpretations. *Hamlet* can be played in innumerable different ways; but it cannot be played any way at all. The same is true of the biblical text.

The third effect of inscription on discourse is that the text now transcends the psycho-sociological conditions of its production. It can now be decontextualized and recontextualized by successive readings as long as there are readers competent to interpret it. These recontextualizations, like diverse settings for a jewel or different environments for a plant or interpretation of a musical score by a different instrument, will exploit the surplus of meaning which the text now has in virtue of its emancipation from authorial intention.

An excellent example of the effect of decontextualization and recontextualization is the ongoing interpretation of the American Declaration of Independence which was written in the patriarchal slave culture of eighteenth century America by adult, white, property-owning, free males. When they wrote that "all men are created equal," they certainly did not intend "men" to include women, blacks, slaves, children, or the poor. Had they been asked, they would have denied emphatically the possibility of equality in personhood and rights of these groups with free, white, adult, propertied males. The proof of this is that amendments to the Constitution were required to extend freedom to slaves and suffrage to women, and Americans have still not passed the Equal Rights Amendment which would extend full equality to women. However, as the founding documents of the republic have been recontextualized throughout the history of the nation, the surplus of meaning of "all men are created equal" has begun to be exploited. In later contexts the humanity of slaves, women, the poor, and children has been progressively acknowledged. In other words, the word "men" has achieved greater extension than the founding fathers could ever have imagined, and thus the predication of equality has extended to new groups of people.

The implications of this theory of text for the reference of a text are enormous. The text, especially a classical text which is so imbued with truth and beauty that it transcends its own era and remains meaningful for successive generations,[19] now refers not merely to the real world of the author, to that which the author intended to express. The text has the capacity to create a world which it projects "in front of itself." This is the possible world which Ricoeur calls "the world in front of the text"[20] as opposed to the world out of which the text came, or the "world behind the text." Although it was derived from the world of the author, the text is no longer limited to reference to that world. Thus, it is not merely informative but has a capacity to function transformatively.

2. Interpreting the Emancipated Text: Transformational Hermeneutics

The text as written discourse looks, as it were, in two directions. It stands between a past world out of which it came and a possible world which it projects. The primary concern of the exegete is to use the text as a kind of "window" onto the past world giving access to the historical setting and experience of the author and his or her contemporaries. Thus, for example, exegesis can reveal the attitudes of first century Christians toward women, the roles women played in the first Christian communities, the theological concerns of the evangelists, and at least a certain amount of data about the historical Jesus. Through the window of the text we glimpse the world of Paul or of the Johannine church.

The primary concern of the hermeneut, however, is with the world in front of the text, the world of possibilities which the text projects before itself. What kind of world does the text create and invite the reader to inhabit? In the case of the New Testament the world the text projects is the world of Christian discipleship. Christian discipleship is community life structured by the paschal mystery of Jesus the Christ. It involves living in hope toward the boundless *shalom* of God according to the pattern of life from death that Jesus established by his cross and resurrection. In other words, the real referent of the New Testament text, what the text is primarily "about," is not the world of first century Christians which we are expected to reconstitute in the twentieth century but the experience of discipleship that is proposed to us and to each successive generation of readers as it was proposed by Jesus to the first generation. The relevant question is not about what roles women played in the Pauline community but about what role women should play in a community of Christian disciples. When Elisabeth Schüssler Fiorenza coined the phrase "a discipleship of equals" to describe the community of Jesus, she was proposing not primarily a description of past Christian experience but the world projected by the New Testament text, the eschatological project which must be realized anew in every age and whose implications will be progressively revealed as the text is recontextualized in successive historical settings.

The competent reader of the classical or normative texts of any community is not first and foremost the individual community member but the community itself.[21] This brings us back to our question about how the judge charged with applying the law to a new case develops the vision necessary to be both faithful to the community's tradition and open to the newness of the contemporary situation. The judge does not function as an autonomous individual deciding what justice and goodness mean and require in each situation. The judge is formed by the community whose values he or she articulates in passing judgment. This does not, of course, mean that justice is determined by majority vote. In fact, part of the basis for the selection of judges is that they are not "reeds shaken in the wind" of popular opinion. But neither are they moral "lone rangers" or judicial monarchs. Judicial wisdom must be distilled from the ongoing experience of the community by the legal processes which utilize both the theoretical developments of jurisprudence and the "common sense," in the strong sense of that term, expressed through such institutions as the Grand Jury and a jury of peers.

In the believing community the interpretation of the biblical text requires a similar community reading which gradually brings to light the meaning of discipleship. One ingredient of this reading is the contribution of biblical scholarship which offers the results of responsible exegesis. But the other ingredient is the experience of Christians, the heirs of two thousand years of lived discipleship. As this community has read and attempted to live the gospel through the centuries, it has become a certain kind of people. Gradually, like Americans seeing the implications for blacks of our foundational commitment to equality, Christians have come to repudiate the slavery which Paul accepted, the potential anti-semitism of Matthew and John, and increasingly the attitude toward war of the Old Testament. In our own day the repudiation of patriarchal oppression of women as it is taught and condoned in the New Testament is arising out of the Christian consciousness of what it means to be called to a discipleship of equals. In other words, the emancipated text is capable of "exploding" the world out of which it came.[22]

This process by which the text produces a people capable of criticizing the text is both a hermeneutical and a dialectical one. It involves not only coming to understand the meaning of discipleship to which we are invited by the text but also allowing this theoretical understanding to be criticized by ongoing praxis.[23] Unless the experience of diminishment and victimization of those for whom the current understanding of discipleship does not work is allowed to challenge that understanding, a closed theory can disguise the ideological distortions of the Christian message by the privileged element in the church structure. It is precisely the experience of women who are marginalized and oppressed in the contemporary church that is challenging the adequacy of our corporate understanding of discipleship. But part of the reason women can and do experience themselves as oppressed in the church is because their experience as disciples of Jesus makes them aware that what is being done to them in the name of God is contrary to the will of Christ for his followers.

V. Engaging the Text from Within

The foregoing analysis of scripture as witness to rather than propositional embodiment of revelation, of text as mediation rather than semantic container of meaning, and of interpretation as transformational appropriation of the world of Christian discipleship rather than unearthing of historical information can, perhaps, open a way for the Christian who is a feminist to engage the biblical text with some hope of liberation. Meaning, according to the theory just proposed, is not equated with or reduced to information about Jesus or the first Christians although this can be useful in the interpretative process. Meaning is, rather, a world of possibility into which the text mediates our entrance. It may, in fact, turn out that the horizon which the text offers to Christian women is finally too constricting. But it is my opinion that the text has not yet been fully engaged from a contemporary hermeneutical and dialectical perspective and therefore that the answer to the question of whether the text is a tool of patriarchy or a resource for women's liberation is not yet available.

If we accept that the witness to God's revelation in Jesus of Nazareth offered to us in the New Testament is the limited, necessarily biased, and sometimes erroneous testimony of believers who, though enjoying a privileged role in the plan of God, were restricted by their personalities, their historical and cultural setting, and their language in both their experience of Jesus and their witness to that experience, then we cannot simply surrender to the text agreeing that what it actually says is precisely what God reveals. On the other hand, if we believe that the text is truly word of God in the sense explained above, then it does have a privileged role in our attempts to engage divine revelation, i.e. to enter into communion with the living God. We cannot, therefore, avoid the arduous task of wrestling with the text in order to engage its meaning, and that wrestling begins necessarily with the exegetical task of grasping what the text actually says. It cannot, however, end there any more than the dialogue with a friend about matters of supreme importance, especially when we seem to disagree, can terminate with ascertaining the literal meaning of the friend's statements on the subject.

Without attempting to be exhaustive I would like to suggest some of the procedures which might be involved in struggling with the text, especially when we are dealing with texts whose content is actually oppressive. First, as Rosemary Ruether has suggested often, the text has to be approached as a whole in light of its own major preoccupations.[24] Liberation of an oppressed people for covenantal life with God is at the heart of the Bible's concerns, and where elements of scripture are incompatible with that concern they must be criticized and sometimes judged simply unfaithful to revelation. To judge that some portion of scripture is not worthy of the God of liberation is not a judgment passed on God but a recognition that our forebears in the faith, those upon whose testimony we depend, were no more infallible than we in understanding and responding to divine revelation. We need not, indeed must not, excise these texts from scripture because their ultimate revelatory purpose may be to alert us to the ways in which Christian experience can go wrong. But we also must not accept as purely and simply the word of God, much less institutionalize in the church, the mistakes of our forebears in the faith.

Second, we must recognize that analogous to the "hierarchy of truths" in systematic theology there is a hierarchy among texts in scripture. To hold that the scriptures as a whole are a foundational witness to divine revelation does not imply equating occasional injunctions or incidental disciplinary regulations or even early Christian teaching with the paschal mystery. It may be that it really does not matter, for contemporary Christians, whether Paul thought that women should be silent in the church. Whatever the value of that injunction in Paul's time (and that needs to be questioned), it is now clear that he was wrong about the appropriateness of women Christians exercising their gifts in the liturgical assembly. This does not solve all problems because it can be excruciatingly difficult to judge particular early Christian practices and teachings in terms of their place within the revelatory framework of Christian life. However, our tradition suggests that nothing, no matter how seemingly sacrosanct, is beyond question. Certainly the decision that the Mosaic law need not be imposed on Gentile converts will never be surpassed in radicality. Ordaining women priests would be far less innovative.

Third, we must enter into the dynamics of the text, or, as Gadamer put it, engage in the question and answer type dialogue which the text initiates.[25] This involves, first of all, the effort to disengage the question to which the text is an answer. When Paul says "women must keep silence in the churches" it is not necessarily to be presumed that he is answering the question, "What is God's will concerning the behavior of women in the church?" Perhaps he is answering the question of disgruntled male Christians, "What are we to do with these obstreperous women who insist on doing things we men have always monopolized?" Or perhaps he is answering the question, "Should we, for the sake of not making ourselves conspicuous, insist that Christian women be bound by the same restrictions that are applied to women in our (i.e. pagan) society?" In each of these cases the meaning of the text as answer would be quite different.

Entering into the dynamics of the text also involves discerning the direction of the answers given, even when the answers themselves fall short of liberating truth. Paul, in the letter to Philemon, actually implicitly legitimates slavery by sending Onesimus, the runaway slave, back to Philemon, his master. But Paul also expresses his dawning awareness that there is something wrong, not necessarily with his decision, but with the situation which necessitated his decision. So he challenges Philemon to receive Onesimus as a brother, not because he must but because that is what Christian faith seems to offer as an ideal. By following the trajectory of Paul's answer we, today, can say firmly that Paul's decision, however prudent in the circumstances or even justified in terms of what was known at the time, must be judged inadequate. Not only can one Christian not hold another Christian a slave but the system of slavery is totally reprehensible not only among Christians but among humans.

Another way of entering into the dynamics of the text involves using the text, not as an apodictic answer to our questions, but as a pedagogical guide for working out our own answers. How did the early Christians struggle with such issues as Mosaic observance, relations with pagans, civil behavior, church order? Maybe what we need to learn from the text is not what we are to do but how we are to go about deciding what to do.

It is also important to try to discern the focus of revelation in problematic texts, i.e. what seems to be radically new and not explainable by the culture in which the text was produced. For example, when the author of Ephesians says that wives are to be subject to their husbands (cf. Eph 5:22) he is not creating Christian teaching, because women in the patriarchal society of that time were necessarily subject to their husbands. But "husbands, love your wives as your own bodies" (cf. Eph 5:28) was new teaching, based explicitly on the implications for Christian marriage relations of understanding the church as the body of Christ. It might be analogous to saying to Christians today, "Of course you should pay your taxes, but make sure you don't support foreign military aggression." The obligation to pay one's taxes is assumed, but something quite new would be injected into the approach to paying taxes if making sure one's taxes were not used for evil purposes were part of that Christian obligation. In fact, it might mean that in some cases one could not pay all of one's taxes. Perhaps, "husbands, love your wives" relativizes essentially "wives, be subject." Is Christian love perhaps as incompatible with unilateral subjection as paying some taxes is with non-cooperation with military aggression?

A fourth way in which we struggle with the text involves bringing to the text questions from our own historical experience which could not possibly have been explicit concerns of first century Christians. Just as the emancipation of slaves was not part of the agenda of the writers of the Declaration of Independence, the morality of nuclear deterrence was utterly beyond the cognitive ken of the New Testament authors. How, then, are we to bring the New Testament to bear upon this ultimately significant modern question? We can only do so by calling into explicit awareness our community grasp of the nature and content of Christian discipleship as it has unfolded over the two thousand years of our lived experience. We cannot find a textual answer to the question, "What does the New Testament say about nuclear arms?" We have to ask what it means to be a Christian and what that implies about nuclear weapons. In other words, we have to deal with modern problems the way the early Christians dealt with issues like the admission of the Gentiles to the church.

A final consideration might be that the history of biblical interpretation in the church suggests that texts can come to function differently from the way they were originally intended to function. The Canticle of Canticles was originally a collection of love songs, and it took centuries for the Jewish community to finally decide that it was to function as an allegory of the relation of God with Israel. Later, the Christian community modified the Jewish canonical decision and began to treat the Canticle of Canticles as an allegory of the relation between Christ and the church or the soul and the word of God.[26] Phyllis Trible in *God and the Rhetoric of Sexuality,* returning to the original meaning of the text as songs celebrating the relationship of human lovers, has shown that the text can function as a corrective to the deformation of the male-female relationship in the course of biblical history.[27] What this suggests is that some texts in scripture might function today not as prescriptions for Christian attitudes or behaviors but as witness to the misunderstanding of the gospel by earlier (or later) Christians.

What all of these procedures for struggling with the biblical text presuppose is that, as readers of scripture from within the community of faith, we are not passive recipients of non-negotiable dicta to which we must submit under penalty of loss of Christian identity. The Christian community is the active subject, not the passive object, of revelation. The biblical text witnesses to revelation, and we engage that witness as criterion of our faith but also as challenge to our own witness. At times we must judge the witness of the scriptures as inadequate, biased, or even counter-evangelical. We do not rewrite the scriptures because no temporal judgment is irreformable and we cannot know what future generations will make of our judgments. Furthermore, even inadequate witness is part of our history and should not be suppressed lest we repeat our errors because we have forgotten them. But we also do not submit passively to the text on the assumption that it conveys without fault or remainder God's explicit intention for the church.

VI. Conclusion

It would be premature to answer the question with which we are engaged, namely whether biblically based Christianity is a viable option for women who claim full and equal personhood within the human and the religious community. What I have tried to suggest is that the question cannot yet be answered definitively in the negative. If we really believe that the word of God is not bound (cf. 2 Tim 2:10) and that the God of universal liberation and *shalom* cannot endorse the oppression of any of God's creatures, then we must find a way to allow God's word to promote and enhance the full personhood of women. Given that the biblical text was written primarily if not exclusively by men in a patriarchal cultural context, this task will not be easy. However, if we as Christians are prepared to abandon both a doctrinal fundamentalism and a scholarly positivism, both of which immure the meaning of the biblical text in an ever more remote and irrelevant past, and undertake a hermeneutical and dialectical project of biblical interpretation which is capable of drawing the text forward out of its past into our present, it may be possible to discover a world of Christian discipleship that is a fit habitation for Christian women. Jesus did not counsel a passive submission to his word, much less to the biblical witness to that word, but an active and progressive engagement of it under the influence of the Spirit who will lead us into all truth (cf. Jn 16:14): "If you continue in my word, you are truly my disciples, and you will know the truth, and the truth will set you free" (Jn 8:32).

3

Feminist Spirituality: Christian Alternative or Alternative to Christianity?

I. Introduction

In the first chapter I attempted to construct a descriptive definition of feminism that was broad enough to embrace most developed versions of feminism that are being espoused and lived at the present time and then to show how feminism is related to the Christian church, especially to the Roman Catholic communion. This relationship was seen to have several dimensions: the participation of the church in the patriarchal oppression of women; the legitimation by the church of the oppression of women in family and society; the struggle of women for full participation as baptized members of the church; and the engagement of the fundamental theological questions about divine revelation concerning God, Christ, and humanity.

In the second chapter we turned to the issue of biblical interpretation to ask how Christians are to understand the special character and role of the Bible in Christian life; what the Bible contributes or can contribute concerning our fundamental questions about God, Christ, and humanity; and, finally, whether and how the Bible can be interpreted so that it can function in the liberation of the very people it has been used to oppress, especially women.

We turn now to the issue of feminism in relation to Christian spirituality, i.e. to the area of lived experience of the faith. It must be noted, however, that the term "spirituality" is no longer an exclusively Christian, nor even an exclusively religious, term. Not surprisingly, therefore, feminist spirituality is not necessarily a Christian or even a religious phenomenon. In fact, however, as we shall see, feminist spirituality whether Christian or not tends to be deeply religious. Consequently, our first task is to define spirituality and specify the meaning of Christian spirituality so that we can then raise the question of how feminism is related to spirituality and finally how feminist spirituality is related to Christian spirituality.

Elsewhere I have traced the history of the term spirituality from its Christian biblical roots as a designation of that which is brought about by the influence of the Holy Spirit, through its development in Christian history to designate primarily the inner life of the Christian striving for more than ordinary holiness, to its contemporary usage not only for religious experience but also for non-religious and even anti-religious life-organizations such as secular feminism and atheistic Marxism.[1] I defined spirituality, as the term is being used today, as "the experience of consciously striving to integrate one's life in terms not of isolation and self-absorption but of self-transcendence toward the ultimate value one perceives."[2] This definition is open enough to include both religious and non-religious life projects but specific enough to exclude aimless spontaneity, partial projects, or religious dilettantism. Its essential elements are conscious effort, the goal of life integration through self-transcendence, and the finalization of the project by ultimate value. Its marked difference from the traditional Christian definition lies in its openness concerning the nature of "ultimate value."

Christian spirituality involves a specification of this definition in terms of the participation of the person in the paschal mystery of Jesus the Christ. For the Christian the horizon of ultimate concern is the holy mystery of God revealed in Jesus Christ and experienced through the gift of the Holy Spirit within the life of the church.[3] Thus, Christian spirituality, as Christian, is essentially trinitarian, christocentric, and ecclesial. Given the way in which the tradition has presented the trinitarian God, viz. as three male "persons," the recent presentation of the theological significance of the maleness of Jesus by the Sacred Congregation for the Doctrine of the Faith,[4] and the church as a hierarchical (i.e. sacralized patriarchal) structure within which women, on the basis of their sex, are excluded from full participation, it is not surprising that women, once their consciousness has been raised, have problems with the living of their faith in terms of the principal coordinates of traditional Christian spirituality. In other words, Christian spirituality will become problematic for any woman who becomes a feminist in the sense in which we have been using the term.

II. Feminism and Spirituality

A. The Background and Development of Feminist Spirituality

The term "feminist spirituality" began to be used very early in the "second wave" of the modern feminist movement, arising in the United States in the 1970s and appearing in Europe in the 1980s.[5] It was mainstreamed in the feminist movement in this country with the publication in 1979 of the groundbreaking work *Womanspirit Rising: A Feminist Reader in Religion,*[6] which was followed ten years later by its sequel, *Weaving the Visions: New Patterns in Feminist Spirituality.*[7]

While some of the feminists using the term spirituality were practicing members of one or another recognized religious tradition, and religion and/or theology was central to the academic feminist interests of most of them, feminist spirituality did not arise within or in terms of any particular institutional church or recognized religion.

Catherina Halkes is probably correct in locating the origin of feminist spirituality not in religion or even in the critique of religion but in the realization by feminists that women's estrangement and oppression are fueled not primarily by sex role polarization but by the dichotomy between spirit and body, with the former assigned to the male and the latter to the female, which is intrinsic to patriarchy.[8] In other words, male control of female sexuality, as it developed over the centuries, led eventually to the identification of women with their sexual/reproductive function and their consequent identification with the realm of the body which led to their gradual exclusion from the realm of the spirit. This spiritual realm, presided over by the male God who reigns in heaven, was opposed to the realm of nature which was relegated to the once universally powerful but now discredited Mother Goddess, the feminine divinity who was finally dethroned and definitively banished by the triumph of patriarchal monotheism.[9]

Feminist spirituality is the reclaiming by women of the reality and power designated by the term "spirit"[10] and the effort to reintegrate spirit and body, heaven and earth, culture and nature, eternity and time, public and private, political and personal, in short, all those hierarchized dichotomous dualisms whose root is the split between spirit and body and whose primary incarnation is the split between male and female.[11]

It is well beyond the scope of this work to enter into the complex and much disputed discussion of how a single, all-powerful male God came to take the place of the Great Goddess and the pantheon of lesser gods and goddesses who were worshiped everywhere in the ancient world before the relatively late advent of patriarchal monotheism in the west.[12] However, certain conclusions from the immense amount of research which has been done on this subject can be accepted as established.

As far back into antiquity as western religion can be traced the supreme deity was female. The Great Goddess was not merely an earth mother, a mate for a male god, or a fertility goddess whose cult justified sexual license. She was the all-powerful Creator, Source of life and of destruction, the Queen of Heaven, the Ruler of the universe. As a number of scholars have argued, this does not prove that there was ever a matriarchal society, a theory for which there is no hard evidence.[13] But even in patriarchal societies in which men controlled the myth and symbol systems, the supreme deity was female and the mediators between the Great Goddess and humans were usually female priests.

Patriarchy, however, was compatible with matrilocal and matrilineal kinship patterns, and strong patriarchal monarchies did not develop until the economic, social, and military conditions for this type of political organization arose. The Israelite monarchy, for example, did not emerge until centuries after the tribes arrived in Canaan, and a major political and military project of the first kings, Saul and David, was to centralize political power. An important aspect of this effort was the unification and centralization of the cult in Jerusalem. David's son Solomon was unable to maintain the fragile unity, and part of his failure to do so was his inability and/or unwillingness to stamp out the religion of the Great Goddess which, in many forms, was alive and well in his kingdom despite the official sanction of Yahwistic monotheism (cf. 1 Kgs 11:1–14).

Gerda Lerner in her very important study *The Creation of Patriarchy* describes the pattern observable in archaic societies which developed strong male monarchies.

> The observable pattern is: first, the demotion of the Mother-Goddess figure and the ascendance and later domination of her male consort/son; then his merging with a storm-god into a male Creator-God, who heads the pantheon of gods and goddesses. Wherever such changes occur, the power of creation and of fertility is transfered [sic] from the Goddess to the God.[14]

In other words, the source of the power of the Goddess, her originating relation to all life, must become the sole possession of the male God if he is to assume unique divinity.[15]

This is precisely the pattern which can be observed in the development of Yahwism. The consolidation of the collection of Hebrew tribes into a single patriarchal monarchy required, as legitimation, patriarchal monotheism. As Elizabeth Dodson Gray says, with compelling clarity:

> When the holy space of a religion is sacred for male sexuality (as in the marking of the covenant upon the male phallus in circumcision), and sacred for blood-sacrifice presided over by males; and when that same holy space is contaminated by female blood and female fertility (as in menstruating and in giving birth), we are dealing with a male fertility cult, no matter what its other lofty spiritual insights may be.[16]

It is not surprising, furthermore, that the second version of the creation myth, the Jahwistic (the so-called J) account in Genesis 2:4b–25 which dates from the early days of the monarchy, presents the creator as a male deity, creating a male human being, from whose side a woman is "born" even though, as everyone knows, all men are actually born from a woman's womb. What is accomplished by the story is the mythical transference of the power of creation and of fertility from Goddess to God and from woman to man. And to put the final seal on the process the woman is then made responsible for the man's moral fall, thus legitimating his dominion over her even though, from creation, she is his equal, "bone of his bone and flesh of his flesh."

The Great Goddess, however, did not die easily in the Hebrew tradition. In fact, she never died completely. In the Old Testament we find not only continual prophetic denunciations of goddess worship (which would not have been necessary if such worship were not prevalent) but also, even in the canonical literature speaking of the one true God of Israel, occasional feminine images of God. In the figure of Holy Wisdom, we have a well-developed feminine personification of God (cf. Wis 8:1–9:6; Wis 6:12–11:1; Prov 8:1–9:12).[17] Nevertheless, there is no question that the Yahwistic commitment to monotheism involved, at least at the human level, a political commitment to patriarchal religion.

To expose the patriarchal political agenda involved in the development of the Jewish religion is not to deny the divinity of the Judaeo-Christian God, the theological truth and importance of monotheism, nor the revelatory character of the biblical text. As Matthew Lamb says in discussing the relation of hermeneutics to dialectics:

> To acknowledge ideological distortions does not imply a total rejection of either faith or science [in our case, feminist historical analysis] in order to find some other 'pure' realm of meaning, nor any lapse into anarchistic incoherence; instead it demands attention to an interpretative heuristics open to dialectical criticism.[18]

But it is to call for a demythologizing of the biblical account for the purpose of distinguishing its patriarchal overlay from its theology of God, its androcentrism from its theology of humanity, and its sexist ideology from its revelatory content just as we must distinguish its scientifically untenable three-tiered cosmology from its doctrine of creation. Monotheism is not necessarily patriarchal any more than Judaism or Christianity is necessarily monarchical. In fact, just as the God of mercy and justice is distorted by the vindictive warrior *persona* assigned to God in some parts of the Old Testament, so the Spirit God who is utterly beyond sex is often deformed by the patriarchal mythology in which the biblical God is usually presented.

The foregoing discussion provides the necessary background for understanding the emergence of contemporary feminist spirituality. Western religion and, in particular, the Judaeo-Christian tradition is deeply patriarchal, not only in its institutional organization but in its theology of God and of humanity. God is presented, not exclusively but overwhelmingly, as a male being. Males, who are perceived to be unequivocally in God's image, are God's representatives and ministers. Women, by virtue of their female sex which is unlike the sex attributed to God, are regarded as deficient images of the divine, unfit to represent God to the worshiping community or minister to him in official cult. Women are subordinate to men, helpers to men in the work of procreation, and thus defined primarily in terms of their sexuality, i.e. their relation to men as wives and mothers, and their participation in the natural processes by which human beings come into existence and thus become subjects of the spiritualization processes over which men preside.

The dichotomous dualism between male divine creator and female natural creation within which the male human is assimilated to the divine sphere and the female human to the natural sphere is the paradigm for the endless series of superior/inferior dichotomies that is characterized as masculine/ feminine. Thus, at the male pole are divine creativity, power, intelligence, initiative, activity, goodness, independence, and at the female pole are natural passivity, weakness, instinct and emotionality, receptivity, evil, dependence. The shorthand cipher for this pervasive dualism is the spirit/body dichotomy, spirit representing everything divine and body representing everything natural. The spirit is male; the body is female. Culture is the triumph of male spirit over female nature.

Feminist spirituality, as we have already noted, began as women reclaiming spirit, refusing to be reduced to body. However, it virtually immediately expanded and deepened to include a reevaluation of body.[19] What feminists in the spirituality movement realized was that the root disorder was not women's confinement to the realm of body but the dichotomy itself which split reality along the spirit/body axis creating an unending and unwinnable war between a supposedly superior spiritual (i.e. male) half of reality and a supposedly inferior bodily (i.e. female) half of reality. They realized that this leads not only to male oppression of females, their exclusion from the realms of "spirit" such as religion, education, politics, and culture, but also to wars between nations struggling to prove their superiority to one another by reducing their enemies to subhuman status, to racial and colonial oppressions of people viewed as intrinsically inferior, and to the mindless rape of the natural environment by man who sees himself as having absolute dominion over nature.

The essence of feminist spirituality, then, is a reclaiming of female power beginning with the likeness of women to the divine, the rehabilitation of the bodily as the very locus of that divine likeness, and the right of women to participate in the shaping of religion and culture, i.e. of the realm of "spirit." This explains the generally religious character of feminist spirituality and, at the same time, its marginality to the mainstream religious traditions which are the principal sources of women's exclusion from the world of "spirit." Against this background we can examine some of the main features of feminist spirituality before looking at the specifically Christian form of the movement.

B. Main Features of Feminist Spirituality

1. Outside the Institutional Context

Feminist spirituality has tended to develop outside the institutional context of either church or academy. This is easily understandable since both these institutions were developed as cultural shrines of the life of the spirit, a life from which women have been excluded, in which they are supposed not to be interested, and for which they have been deemed unequipped. Thus the rituals and texts of religion as well as the research techniques, the canon of classical texts, and the teaching methods of the academy include very little of women's experience or history and even less that would be empowering of women. There is little place for women or for the experience or exercise of feminine power in either church or academy. In fact, a major function of both institutions has been to restrict women to the private sphere, the domestic environment, the ancillary roles, while power was possessed and exercised by men. The economic arrangements which support both church and academy are such that funding is usually not available for so-called "alternative"

projects, i.e. for projects that fall outside the patriarchal interests already in place.[20]

Consequently, feminist spirituality both in theory and in
practice has developed on the fringes of institutional culture.
This allows feminists a certain freedom to tell their individual
and corporate stories which are mutually empowering and
to experiment with new theories that are *anathema* in the
academy and new rituals which seem frivolous or shocking
to mainstream religion. However, it has also kept scholars in
feminist spirituality both from the variety and scope of critical exchange in the academy that would profit both women
feminist scholars and their non-feminist dialogue partners
and from full participation in their respective religious traditions which would be empowering for feminists and purify-
ing and enriching for their churches.

2. The Discovery of Goddess[21]

An aspect of feminist spirituality which is most disturbing to mainline religion is discourse about Goddess. No
doubt there is a deep, visceral awareness, especially among
the guardians of patriarchal religion, that the reemergence of
the goddess is potentially the greatest conceivable threat to
the religious status quo. However, because of the importance
of the Goddess theme, no discussion of feminist spirituality
which avoids this issue can be even minimally adequate.

Basically, Goddess is the symbol of female divinity, i.e.
of feminine sacred power, just as God is the symbol of male
divinity or masculine sacred power. There are two main questions about the symbol for divinity: Is the divinity symbolized
in masculine or feminine form actually male or female? How
are real males and females related to the divinity? Various
strands of feminist spirituality answer these questions dif-

ferently. Three of these strands are of major significance for an understanding of feminist spirituality.

Thealogy: The most radical form of feminist spirituality involves the worship of the Great Mother Goddess who is conceived of as the one, true, ultimate divinity.[22] The study of her nature and her relations with creation and humanity is called the*a*logy, i.e. discourse about Goddess, rather than theology or discourse about God. However, a major difference between the understanding of Goddess in thealogy and of God in theology is that Goddess is conceived as ultimately immanent rather than ultimately transcendent. More exactly, her transcendence is her all-embracing, all-empowering immanence. She is transcendently immanent. Thus, Goddess not only divinizes the feminine and its life-giving mysteries but also negates the ruinous split between transcendent and immanent, spirit and body, divinity and nature, heaven and earth with all their Manichean progeny in the realms of thought and action. A feminine deity allows women to experience themselves as truly "like Goddess," as imaging divinity in their very life-giving powers. Rather than being unclean because of their bodily capacity to give life, they are divine because of it. Women are rehabilitated in the rehabilitation of the body which is not the opposite of spirit but the enspirited vessel of divine creativity.

Closely related to Goddess religion and spirituality but not necessarily identical with it is the revitalization of Wicca, or pre-Christian, European traditions of pagan religion.[23] The deity of these nature religions is female and her devotees are predominantly although not exclusively women. They come together in "covens" and often call themselves "witches," a deliberately provocative practice which not only intends to unmask the irrational male fear of female religious power but also to expiate the murder of millions of women throughout

Christian history who have been executed on the charge of witchcraft.[24]

Witchcraft is not the "black magic" or nocturnal sexual orgies feared by the religious establishment but a ritual participation in the life-giving and healing powers of nature which are seen as divine. For Wicca, which means "wisdom" or the "wise ones," the universe is not an inert thing but a living reality in which everything is intimately interconnected. Human beings are the priestesses of creation, not its lords. Spirituality includes sexuality without being either reduced to it or dominant over it. Life and love are supreme values which are not at odds with truth. Ritual plays a very important role in witchcraft because it is the place where spirit and nature meet and interact, sacralizing all of reality and uniting us to ourselves, to one another, and to the universe.[25]

God/dess: A less radical form of feminist spirituality, and one with whose approach to divinity many Christian feminists are much more comfortable, is well symbolized by respelling the verbal symbol of divinity as G-o-d / d-e-s-s. What such women are doing is appropriating for women all that is true in the theological and religious tradition about God. While repudiating the patriarchal and masculinizing deformation of the God-tradition, they continue to relate to the deity of Judaeo-Christian revelation. They emphasize the feminine aspects of the biblical deity, insist on a compensatory highlighting of feminine biblical metaphors for Yahweh, demand the use of gender inclusive language for both divine and human being in prayer and worship, and struggle toward a reimagining, for themselves and others, of the male God in female terms. In other words, they refuse to allow the biblical God to be appropriated by men and used against women. They see themselves as fully in the image and likeness of God/dess, not only because they possess intellect and will,

i.e. spiritual faculties, but also because they participate bodily in the great divine work of giving and nurturing life. Thus
they attempt to achieve much the same appropriation of
spiritual power, rehabilitation of the body, and reintegration
of the dichotomized spheres of reality that more radical
Goddess worshippers do, but they seek to do this without
separating themselves from the Judaeo-Christian biblical and
sacramental tradition.[26]

**Therapeutic or Psychological Approach to the
Goddesses:** A third way in which feminist spirituality has
incorporated the goddess is basically psychological and therapeutic. Basing themselves on the archetypal theory of Carl
Jung, but repudiating or modifying Jung's animus/anima
dichotomy, some feminist psychotherapists have seen the
potential of goddess archetypes for healing the profound
self-hatred and self-rejection which patriarchal culture has
inculcated in women by teaching them to identify with the
inferior qualities regarded as "feminine" while assigning
the superior human qualities to men.[27] Jung recognized the
potentiality of transcultural intrapsychic patterns, which he
called archetypes, to constellate the complexes of thought
and feeling which are operative in our daily experience. A
fundamental pair of archetypes, according to Jung, are the
anima or the feminine principle in the male psyche, and the
animus or the male principle in the female psyche.

The major problem with Jung's theory, from a feminist
perspective, is that Jung assigned the culturally stereotypical
masculine qualities, i.e. those associated with spirit such as
logical reason, initiative, creativity, etc., to the masculine
principle and the culturally stereotypical feminine qualities,
i.e. those associated with body, such as emotion, instinct,
receptivity, passivity, etc., to the feminine principle. The net
result was that men were enabled to draw upon the resources

of the dark, inferior, and less differentiated feminine qualities which, in small doses, make life richer, more exciting,
and more beautiful without ever having to identify with
them, whereas women could reach above themselves into
the higher sphere of spirit, mind, and creativity but could
never claim these qualities as their own. They would always
experience these qualities as recessive in themselves, foreign
to their true nature, borrowed for special occasions when
they had to act in spheres not their own, e.g. in the academy,
political life, or religious leadership. Despite Jung's effort to
valorize both the feminine and the masculine, his dichotomous approach had the effect of canonizing the traditional
sexual stereotypes and the cultural hierarchizing of masculine and feminine which alienates women from the realm
of "spirit."

Feminist Jungian psychotherapists have revised the
schema by agreeing that there are indeed archetypes of the
masculine and the feminine in the psyche but that they are
multiple.[28] Women have a plurality of archetypes of the feminine within themselves as men have a plurality of masculine
archetypes. Using the ancient Greek goddesses to describe
the archetypes of the feminine in women, these therapists
have explained the ascendency in certain women, or in the
same woman under different circumstances, of the inner par-
adigms not only of mother, child, and wife but also of solitary
huntress, warrior and strategist, alchemical lover, contemplative virgin, goal-focused achiever, leader, thinker, intellectual
mentor, artist, craftsperson, spiritual guide, and so on. Neither the bodily nor the spiritual is either more or less "natural" in women. The spiritual does indeed have a feminine
persona in a woman, but it is not a recessive masculinity. It is
her own feminine power active in a sphere from which real
women have been traditionally excluded. The psychological

task of women is to actualize all the inner goddesses, all the archetypes of female power.

3. Salient Characteristics of Feminist Spirituality

Against this background it is fairly easy to identify the salient characteristics of feminist spirituality and to see their interconnections. First, feminist spirituality is both rooted in and oriented toward *women's experience,* especially their experiences of disempowerment and of empowerment. For this reason story-telling, the narratizing and sharing of the experience of women which has been largely excluded from the history of mainline religion, is central.[29] Story-telling is both a technique for consciousness-raising and a source of mutual support. By telling their own stories women appropriate as significant their own experience which they have been taught to view as trivial. By listening to the stories of other women they come to see the commonalities and the political power in women's experience which they have been taught to believe is purely personal and private.

Second, as we have already seen, feminist spirituality is deeply concerned with the reintegration of all that has been dichotomized by patriarchal religion. This involves rehabilitating what has been regarded as inferior and reappropriating that which has been alienated. The fundamental reintegration is that of body with spirit. Thus, feminist spirituality is concerned with giving voice to and celebrating those aspects of *bodiliness* which religion has covered with shame and silence, particularly those feminine experiences associated with life-giving which have been reduced to sex and those aspects of sexuality which have been regarded as unclean.[30]

Very closely related to the emphasis on the goodness and holiness of the body is a third characteristic, a profound *concern with non-human nature.* Feminist theorists have explicated exhaustively the intimate connection between male possessiveness and exploitative violence toward women and that same possessiveness and exploitative violence toward nature. As men have raped women for their own pleasure and utility, so have they raped the environment for the same purposes. Feminists are convinced that only a spirituality which values both women and all those elements of the universe that have been "feminized," including nature, children, the poor, the disabled, the aged, and the infirm, can contribute to a renewed and livable world.[31]

A fourth characteristic of feminist spirituality is its rejection of cerebral, rationalistic, and abstract approaches to religious participation. The emphasis on *ritual* that is participative, circular, aesthetic, incarnate, communicative, life-enhancing, and joyful is a deliberate rejection of the rigidly unemotional, overly verbal, hierarchical, and dominative liturgical practice of the mainline churches. And feminists choose to organize themselves religiously not in the hierarchical institutional structures of patriarchal religion with its insistence on obedience and conformity but in communities that are inclusive and participative. Consequently, feminists involved in the spirituality movement are committed to a reenvisioning of ministry, liturgy, theology, teaching, community building, and ecclesiastical organization.

A final, but perhaps the most important, characteristic of feminist spirituality is that from the very beginning it has involved commitment to the intimate and intrinsic *relationship between personal growth and transformation and a politics of social justice.*[32] The feminist rallying cry, "the personal is political," means not only that the problems women have experienced as their personal and private concerns are actually systemically caused and can only be rectified through structural reform, but also that societal transformation is only possible through and on the basis of personal transformation. Thus, unlike the traditional spiritualities of the churches which constantly (and often unsuccessfully) seek a point of intersection between a process of personal spiritual growth and a commitment to social justice, feminist spirituality starts with a commitment which faces simultaneously inward and outward. The changes and growth which must happen in women if they are to be and to experience themselves as fully human, daughters of divinity and its bearers in this world, are the same changes that must occur in society, namely, the reintegration of what has been dichotomized, the empowerment of that which has been marginalized and abused, the liberation of that which has been enslaved.

The word which has progressively come to serve as a cipher for feminist spirituality is "interconnectedness." In every area feminists involved in the spirituality movement are seeking ways to reunify everything that has been divided by the all-pervasive dichotomous dualism of the patriarchal system, to replace the win-lose, either-or, we-they, in-out, right-wrong bases of mutual destruction with a both-and inclusiveness which will both achieve and be achieved by reconnecting that which has been separated. Feminist spirituality prefers networks to chains of command, webs to ladders, circles and mosaics to pyramids, and weaving to building.[33] It wants discourse to be both rational and affective, dialogue to replace coercion, cooperation rather than competition to be our usual mode of operation, power to be used for empowerment rather than mastery, persuasion to take the place of force, and all of this to be not merely the way individuals function but the way society functions. In short, feminist spirituality is a commitment to bringing about, in oneself and in the world, that alternative vision which is integral to feminism as a comprehensive ideology.

III. Feminist Spirituality and Christian Spirituality

We come finally to the question of the relationship of Christian women and men who are feminists to feminist spirituality. Certain tensions, and also many points of convergence, should already have become obvious. However, just as there is considerable diversity among secular and post-Christian religious feminists involved in feminist spirituality, so Christians who are feminists occupy a variety of positions on a continuum running from very traditional Christian spirituality to very revisionist approaches. One way to distinguish among Christians who are feminists and who are involved in feminist spirituality is to examine the points of departure from which various feminists have come to identify themselves with the spirituality movement.

A. *Varieties of Christian Feminist Spirituality*

Not all women's spirituality is feminist just as not all women's movements are feminist. It is entirely possible for women to have a very patriarchal spirituality. In fact, it may well be the case that the spirituality of most women in the church is still at least unreflectively if not militantly patriarchal. However, there are women who claim the designation of feminist for spiritualities which most feminists would not recognize as such and might even consider anti-feminist.

Sometimes the designation feminist is simply an anachronism, a matter of assigning the term feminist to a woman who had a positive spiritual self-image and maintained her integrity in the face of patriarchal power.[34] Sometimes the term is appropriated by women who exalt the role in their religious experience of precisely those qualities, such as receptivity and passivity, which men have devalued and assigned to women. Sometimes people simply equate the spirituality of women, especially insofar as it seems to contrast with the spirituality of men, with feminist spirituality.

As has been said in relation to feminism itself, feminist spirituality is necessarily informed by a developed feminist consciousness which is quite different from a positive self-image as a woman or even a basic commitment to the well-being of women. Feminist consciousness begins in an appropriated and criticized experience of sexual oppression and involves a critique of patriarchy as the cause of that oppression, an alternative vision of a non-patriarchal future, and a commitment to structural change to realize that vision.

A first group of Christians whose spirituality is genuinely feminist are people who have been deeply involved with personal and/or social spirituality within the Christian tradition and who came to feminist consciousness at some point and began to realize that it had serious implications for their spiritual life.[35] Many Catholic religious women and other ministers have had this experience. They have become sensitized to the oppressive masculinity of the language of prayer and celebration and the way that this linguistic hegemony functions to legitimate and reinforce ecclesiastical patriarchy. They are estranged from a male God in whose likeness they cannot imagine themselves and who is, for all practical purposes, men-writ-large. They have become progressively alienated from a sacramental system in which males exercise sacred power over women to grant or deny access to God and use sacramentally based office to exclude women from full participation in the church. They have come to recognize the ways in which male-controlled theology, moral formation, and spiritual guidance have functioned to infantilize and demonize women. In short, their consciousness-raising has extended to the sphere of spirituality and they have begun to judge traditional Christian spirituality as seriously flawed, even destructive of women.[36]

A second type of Christian feminist is the person whose coming to feminist spirituality began in her or his involvement in feminist liberationist praxis.[37] As this person has grown in awareness of the ways in which women are marginalized, excluded, victimized, degraded, and oppressed in family and society, he or she has begun to see that women undergo the same oppression in the church and that the church is a major legitimator of the oppression of women in family and society. The social analysis which enables such people to identify patriarchy as the root of women's social, economic, and political oppression is extended to the church where it is identified as the cause of women's religious oppression. However, such people recognize that the situation in the church is complicated by the spiritual element. It is not merely that the church as social institution is patriarchal but that patriarchy has infected the inner life of the church as a community. Sexual apartheid in the church, like racial apartheid in South Africa, is not just an evil social structure but a deadly cancer of the spirit which is destroying not only its intended victims, women, but all believers whose spiritual experience is patriarchally deformed.

A third type of Christian who becomes interested in feminist spirituality is the woman who has experienced personal oppression and violence in the church. She may be a religious whose congregation's constitutional revision process has been violated or who has been threatened with serious sanctions for exercising her basic human rights; a married woman enraged by church law on contraception, divorce, or abortion formulated by male celibates without any input from those who bear the brunt of those decisions; a woman in ministry who has been summarily fired without explanation from a post she has filled with distinction for many years because the new pastor is not comfortable with women; a woman seminary student who cannot accept that her vocation to priestly ministry is simply denied without testing on the basis of her sex; a wife who completes the diaconate formation program with her husband who is then ordained while she is quietly dropped from consideration; a woman who is raising the child she conceived with a priest who continues to function in good standing while she bears the onus of single parenting and the ecclesial opprobrium of adultery; a parent whose child has been sexually molested by a cleric who is protected by the system. This type of experience, because it is so personally painful and is inflicted by church officials who claim to be acting in the name of God, frequently creates a crisis in the spirituality of the victims. They can no longer relate to the God who is presented and represented in this way and they are forced, through a crisis of faith, to find a new approach to God or even a new God to approach.

A fourth type of Christian feminist is the person who has become involved in the secular or post-Christian feminist spirituality movement and gradually finds it more satisfying, more life-giving, than participation in traditional patriarchal church life. She may continue to go to mass on Sunday and try to pray as before, but she finds herself overcome with anger at the sexist language of the liturgy and the unrelieved maleness of ministry; she can no longer read or listen to the paternalistic pronouncements of the hierarchy exhorting her to accept with humble joy her second class status in the church; she is unable to read or meditate on a biblical text that suppresses her history and violates her sense of self-worth; ministering under the domination of clerics is becoming intolerable. Little by little she finds herself identifying with the community of feminists with whom she celebrates inclusive and empowering rituals and disassociating herself from the oppressive experiences of mainline Christian spirituality.

In summary, women who are both Christian and feminist come to see the relevance of feminism to their Christian spirituality in a number of different ways. For some, feminist insight comes as an addition to and an enrichment of a basically traditional experience of growth in the Christian spiritual life. For others, their feminist consciousness, raised in other circumstances or in relation to other issues, begins to enlighten their Christian spirituality and to call into question the assumptions of that spirituality insofar as these are patriarchal and oppressive. Others come to feminist spirituality out of an experience of ecclesiastical oppression, and still others out of an alienation that is intensified by its contrast with liberating feminist experience. What all of these paths have in common is that they lead directly into the area of spirituality, i.e. they touch not just institutional participation but the lived experience of the faith, the intimate place where the human person encounters the Holy Mystery of being, life, and love. This is why the issue of feminist spirituality is for most Catholic women whose consciousness has been raised a much more serious issue than questions of institutional reform. It raises questions of whether the God of the Judaeo-Christian tradition can be God for a self-respecting woman; whether Jesus is a savior or an oppressor of women; whether sacraments can be experienced as symbolic encounters with God or only as the sacred ritualization of male domination; whether one can find oneself as a person and grow healthily in a community in which one's personhood and Christianity will never be fully recognized. The agony of the Catholic who is a feminist is experienced primarily in the area of spirituality.

B. *Responses to the Effect of Feminism on the Spirituality of Catholics*

No matter how the Catholic woman who is a feminist comes to see the connection between her feminism and her Catholic spirituality, seeing the connection will present at the very least a major challenge in the area of faith life and in all probability a major crisis.

One response to the crisis, and one which is becoming, unfortunately, ever more common, is abandonment of the Christian tradition. Raised feminist consciousness makes the person simply unable to absorb the incessant spiritual abuse of a resolutely patriarchal institution and she opts for her personhood, her self-respect, and her continuing spiritual growth which she realizes cannot be pursued in such an oppressive environment. Such feminists often refer to themselves as post-Christian, indicating that their roots are in the Christian tradition and that their feminist position is not neutral in relation to that tradition. But they no longer consider themselves Christians and no longer recognize the claim of the Christian community or institution upon them.

The responses with which I am most concerned in this chapter, however, are those of feminists who do not leave, or at least have not yet left the institution even though many of these admit that remaining is a daily painful choice. There seem to be at least two general groups of women who are both Christian and feminist: 1) those who are basically within the mainstream of the Christian tradition and whose spirituality remains recognizably Christian but who are involved in a continuous and radical criticism of the tradition; 2) those who are still formally within the institutional church but who have, to a large extent, relocated their spirituality into what has been named "womenchurch." These two groups are by no means totally distinct, and most Christian women who are feminists probably have some affiliation with both. I am distinguishing them for the sake of clearer description and analysis.

1. Mainstream: Feminist Catholics

For purposes of clarity I will call the first group "feminist Catholics," making Catholic the substantive and feminist a modifier. These feminists are usually women who have spent most of their lives developing a personal spirituality within the Catholic Christian tradition. Theirs is not a purely institutional spirituality, a matter of accepting church teaching, keeping church laws, and "practicing the faith" according to current church norms.

These women, many of whom are or were members of religious congregations, have developed a deep personal prayer life nourished by prolonged meditation on the scriptures that has formed in them a Christ-consciousness which is now integral to their personalities. Often this Christ-consciousness has been deeply marked by a personally appropriated study of one or another of the church's great spiritual traditions and/or personalities, such as Benedictine liturgical spirituality or Teresian contemplative spirituality. These women responded with spiritual joy and enthusiasm to the renewal of sacramental and liturgical life in the conciliar period and were delighted to replace the somewhat wooden and impersonal preached retreats of their youth with intense experiences of personal growth in solitary directed retreats. Spiritual vitality overflowed in their adult years in committed and energetic ministry which became more and more creative as the decline in numbers of clergy and a renewed ecclesiology conspired to open previously clerical ministries to the non-ordained.

In short, the feminists in this first group are people with mature, personally appropriated spiritualities. Their spirituality was born within and nourished by the Catholic tradition. Jesus is central to their faith life which is trinitarian and communal, and their ministry is an integral expression of their spiritual lives. Christianity, specifically in its Catholic incarnation, is not merely an institutional affiliation of which they can divest themselves like a person leaving her country club, or an ideological commitment which one might lay aside by conviction like a Marxist leaving the Communist Party, or even a cherished vocation which one might surrender for a greater good like a teacher retiring in order to raise a child. These people do not *belong* to the Catholic Church; they *are* Catholics. And their Catholic identity is constituted much more by their spirituality, their lived experience of the faith, than by institutional affiliation. Even if these feminists chose to sever their institutional connection they would find it virtually impossible to de-Catholicize their spirituality because Catholicity constitutes that spirituality in a fundamental way.

While it is certainly not possible to give a single description of the spiritual journey of such a large and diverse group of people, it might be possible to suggest, in a general way, the effect of heightened feminist consciousness on such women and the ways in which the encounter of their two commitments, viz. Catholicism and feminism, influences their spirituality. One way to organize this description is to talk of the inner and the outer faces of the experience.

Feminist consciousness, once raised, can only deepen. Consciousness-raising makes it impossible to ever "go home again." Once sensitized to the reality and the effects of patriarchy, one can only become ever more aware of its pervasiveness, more convinced of its destructiveness, more resistant to its influence on oneself and one's world. The feminist Catholic may begin with a mildly disturbing realization that the religious language of her tradition is heavily sexist, that she is being victimized in her ministry by the irrational fear and hatred of women that has been bred into an all-male, celibate clergy, that the God-imaging in the tradition is overwhelmingly masculine, that she is being restricted in totally unnecessary ways in the exercise of her sacramental life because of her sex. But once she has begun to see, begun the critical process of analysis, she will necessarily gradually be overwhelmed by the extent, the depth, and the violence of the institutional church's rejection and oppression of women. This precipitates the inward crisis which the feminist Catholic inevitably faces: a deep, abiding, emotionally draining anger that, depending on her personality, might run the gamut from towering rage to chronic depression.

This experience, which must be distinguished from the episodic anger we all experience in the face of frustrations or everyday mistreatment, should probably be called existential anger. It is not a temporary emotion but a state of being. Members of oppressed races and social classes know this experience well. Waking up in the morning angry and going to bed at night angry, especially for a person who has been socialized to women's responsibility for keeping peace in family and community and who has learned from childhood that a good Christian does not even feel, much less express anger, is a personally shattering experience. There are no categories or techniques in the repertoire of Christian spirituality for understanding or dealing with existential anger.[38]

The onslaught of existential anger faces the feminist Catholic with a new and all-embracing spiritual agenda for which the tradition offers little help. The data of the experience are conflicting. In her heart the feminist Catholic knows that her anger is not only justified but mandatory, just as was Jesus' anger at the oppressive hypocrisy of the clergy of his day, but this does not allay the guilt that arises from a lifetime of socialization and indoctrination about the unacceptability of this passion. At some deep level she believes in the Catholic faith tradition, but she sees more and more clearly that every aspect of it is not just tainted but perverted by the evil of patriarchy. It is not that the tradition has some problems; the tradition is the problem. She wants to hope that institutional purification and conversion are possible, but there is very little evidence that the male guardians of the patriarchal establishment have any intention of even addressing the problem. She wishes she could focus her anger on institutional arrangements and doctrinal positions, but the source of her suffering and the cause of her anger are most often real people, usually males in power positions who really cannot be honestly excused on the grounds of stupidity or ignorance because they *do* know what they are doing. These people are simultaneously her personal oppressors and those for whose salvation Jesus died.

Not only are the data of the situation conflicting but the behavioral alternatives, at times, are all simultaneously unacceptable or ineffective. Walking out of offensive liturgies not only deprives her of sacramental experience but usually has little effect on the offending presider; but remaining only enrages her and confirms the offender in his oppressive practice. Expressing her anger to males who are sufficiently sensitized to the issue to understand what she is saying risks alienating potential allies; but expressing it to those who most need to hear it is a waste of time; and not expressing it at all is psychologically dangerous. Furthermore, the institutional powers are in agreement that a woman accused of "being angry," like the woman once accused of "being a witch," can be disposed of with impunity. Thus, expressing her anger can cost her her job, her reputation, and any leverage she might have for bringing about change, while repressing her anger destroys her own integrity and psychological balance and makes her an accomplice in the oppression of her sisters.

While these descriptions are indicative rather than exhaustive, they should suffice to make the point. The feminist Catholic is in the sociological position in the church of the person of color in South African society. Sexual apartheid works exactly like racial apartheid. Oppression, frustration, discouragement, and hopelessness fuel an existential anger that is overwhelming, unquenchable, and utterly exhausting. The spiritual agenda of the feminist Catholic often consists primarily in searching for some constructive way to deal with existential anger, to become in her own way a spiritual Nelson Mandela or Rosa Parks or Joan of Arc.

A Carmelite, Constance FitzGerald, in a widely read article entitled "Impasse and the Dark Night,"[39] has suggested a way of conceptualizing, in the mystical categories of the Carmelite contemplative tradition, the experience of being totally blocked that is central to the existential anger of many feminist Catholics. Carolyn Osiek, in her book *Beyond Anger*,[40] has tried to suggest ways to both affirm the anger and to use it without becoming paralyzed by it. Elsewhere I have suggested that women's experience might be a resource for a renewed theology of the cross[41] as well as for an appropriation of ministerial gifts.[42]

These psychological and spiritual resources, some explicitly Christian and religious, some therapeutic, some sociological, are gradually emerging as feminist Catholics share their experiences of alienation and search for a way out. Two major fora for this sharing that have proved immensely strengthening for many feminist Catholics are spiritual direction, especially with a feminist woman director,[43] and support groups in which women come together to strengthen one another in suffering, to strategize for change, and to celebrate both traditional Catholic liturgies and alternative rituals. Their experience is not unlike that of the earliest Jewish Christians who, while continuing to participate in temple and synagogue, also met together in their homes to share and celebrate their Christian identity and faith which could not find expression in the Jewish assembly. Years of intense living of Christian spirituality has strengthened these women in their conviction that there are resources within them for living even the passion and crucifixion of ecclesial patriarchy and that resurrection is worth their hope.

The outward expression of feminist Catholic spirituality usually takes the form of active commitment to ecclesiastical reform. Many of these women are active in the Women's Ordination Conference, Catholics Speak Out, the Association for the Rights of Catholics in the Church, Mary's Pence, and other groups involved in ongoing challenge to the institution. Often they serve as well on diocesan pastoral councils, associations of religious and/or lay women, and advisory groups to church leaders.

Feminist Catholics in the academy are involved in a full-scale revisionist criticism of the Catholic tradition. Women scholars in church history, pastoral theology, biblical studies, systematic theology, sacramental theology, and moral theology are creating an alternative body of theological reflection which serious theologians can no longer ignore.[44] They are demonstrating that what has been blithely regarded as "the tradition" of the church is, at most, half the tradition. Church history is not the history of the church but of what men have preserved of male experience for male purposes. Much that the hierarchy would like to present as simply "theology" is the local theology of those in power often developed for ideological ends. Biblical interpretation has been done almost exclusively by exegetes wearing, unconsciously but really, sexual blinders. And while moral theology has been developed by male celibates unenlightened by the contribution of at least half of those who lived that morality, pastoral theology has been distorted by the exclusion of the ministerial experience of half the church.

Feminist Catholics, especially those directly involved in pastoral ministry, are pouring immense energy into the reform of life in the grassroots communities of the church. They are refusing to tolerate gender exclusive language in daily discourse or liturgical celebration; they are taking effective action, sometimes even legal action, to protect their rights against clerical privilege and the arbitrary use of hierarchical power; they are changing the dominative procedures of the ecclesiastical workplace in the direction of feminist models of cooperation and participation; they are building alternative models of religious community.

Feminist Catholic parents and teachers are committed to raising the next generation of Catholics as feminists. They want the boys they deal with to eschew anything, including the ordained ministry, from which their sisters are excluded. They want girls to recognize their exclusion whenever and wherever it occurs and to protest it loudly and effectively. Above all, they want the girls and boys they are raising and educating to experience themselves as equals and to treat each other that way so that there will not be replacements for the generation of patriarchs that is dying.

What all of this activity has in common is that it is constructive expenditure of energy for the transformation of the church. Not only does it channel the existential anger with which feminist Catholics wrestle interiorly, but it is having an effect. The concerns of feminists can no longer be trivialized or ignored by church officials.[45] Although it often seems that no progress has been made and no change seems likely, the extent and depth of change is actually astounding when one realizes that the Catholic feminist movement is less than thirty years old. Institutional arrangements have not been modified in any significant way. But the foundations on which those arrangements rest have been seriously undermined and the flow of personnel, money, and commitment necessary to sustain those arrangements is drying up. Like the Berlin Wall and South African apartheid, the church's patriarchal sexism appears immovable, but it is built on the sand of oppression, and history is on the side of liberation and justice.

2. Womenchurch

A second group of women who are both feminist and Catholic are those we might call Catholic feminists. Here the substantive is feminist and the adjective is Catholic. The primary social location and focus of personal commitment of these women is to feminism, and this is what characterizes and determines the extent and the quality of their participation in the Catholic tradition. Most of these women find their spiritual home not in Catholic parishes or alternative communities but in the movement called "Womenchurch."[46]

Womenchurch defines itself as church, i.e. as a community of religiously engaged and motivated people who are women-identified. Their starting point is the experience of women, not any particular institutional religious tradition, although the movement originated among Catholic women moving beyond the goal of ordination into a self-understanding as an exodus community, a community not in exile from the church in sectarianism or schism but the community of church in exodus from patriarchy. Their goal is the full personhood of women, not the maintaining or improving of the religious institution or the saving of disincarnate souls, their own or anyone else's. The criterion by which they judge the genuinely religious quality of any experience, project, or process is whether it is life-giving for women.

Women in the Womenchurch movement now come from many different religious traditions, Christian and other, and from no tradition, although most of its members probably are or were originally Catholic and most Catholic women in the movement remain Catholics. Many Catholic women who experience themselves primarily as feminists but who have not abandoned institutional affiliation with Catholicism find themselves most at home in Womenchurch settings. And many feminist Catholics, such as those described in the previous section, participate in and are nourished by Womenchurch events even though their primary religious affiliation remains the institutional church.

The spirituality of Womenchurch is essentially feminist spirituality rather than the spirituality of mainline Christianity. Consequently, Womenchurch easily brings together for story-sharing, analysis, strategizing, political action, and ritual feminists who share a deep concern for religion but no common ecclesiastical or cultural history. Catholics, Protestants, Buddhists, native Americans, and devotees of pagan Wicca; whites and women of color; ordained women, lay women, and women religious all come together in Womenchurch on the basis of shared feminist theory and praxis which is the fundamental shaper of the reflection, action, and ritual of the community.

We might illustrate the difference between feminist Catholics and Catholics in Womenchurch as follows. A group of feminist Catholics might celebrate eucharist without an ordained presider but they would probably use the basic format of Catholic eucharist and they would be concerned about the question of how their celebration is related to the sacramental tradition of the church. A group of Catholic feminists at a Womenchurch event, if they chose to celebrate eucharist (which is less likely because they would have trouble with its patriarchal presuppositions no matter who presided and because they would be unlikely to be in an all-Catholic group), would probably not be concerned with that question. They would be much more likely to develop a ritual, perhaps involving the sharing of a communal meal of bread and wine, which they would not see themselves as "borrowing" from a male church which owns the sacraments but would see as an organic expression of their own power to celebrate their spirituality.

Characteristic, then, of Catholic feminists is their primary self-location in the church of women, i.e. Womenchurch, whatever other institutional religious affiliations they might maintain. Second, their spirituality is essentially feminist rather than Christian or non-Christian, although it is usually enriched by those elements of the Catholic tradition which they still find meaningful. Its primary characteristics are those we discussed above under the heading of feminist spirituality, viz. non-institutional location, rootedness in women's experience rather than ecclesiastical tradition, a profound concern to rehabilitate the bodily while reclaiming the spirit for women and thus healing the dichotomous dualisms characteristic of patriarchy, ecological sensitivity, a deep commitment to social transformation as integral to personal transformation, and a concern that all of their interaction be characterized by interconnectedness expressed in full participation, circularity of organization and shared leadership, artistic beauty, inclusiveness, and joy.

Catholic feminists, along with religiously committed feminists from other traditions, are not content to await, actively or passively, the reform of the institutional church. They have undertaken to develop rituals which not only do not oppress them but will give them life and hope. They do not hesitate to rewrite the stories of the tradition from the standpoint of women's experience, to repudiate the stories from the tradition which marginalize, demonize, or degrade women, and to write new stories which carry the non-patriarchal content of the tradition in ways that are meaningful for women.[47] These feminists are also not waiting for the institutional church to ask for their opinion about or to reform the official positions on moral matters that affect women. They are not controlled by guilt in relation to the institution, and many have taken anti-establishment positions on such issues as contraception, divorce and remarriage, homosexuality, and abortion. In short, they are busy *being* church rather than trying to reform the male establishment which is usually regarded as church. However, they both hope for and expect that men of good will will eventually join them in the reshaping of a church for all believers. Thus their separatism is neither total nor ideological but practical and provisional, although no one in the movement thinks that the reintegration will happen anytime soon.

C. Catholic and Feminist: The Future of Women's Spirituality in the Catholic Church

While some women who are both Catholic and feminist could locate themselves clearly in one or the other of the two positions described above, many others would find it very difficult to do so. Depending on the situation, the issue, the occasion, or the participants, they would identify primarily with their Catholic tradition or primarily with their feminist affiliation. Against the background of the descriptions given above I would suggest two conclusions about the future of women's spirituality in the Catholic Church.

1. Complementarity of Feminist Catholicism and Catholic Feminism

First, feminist Catholics and Catholic feminists are making a complementary contribution to the transformation of both Catholic spirituality and the institutional church. In the area of spirituality it seems clear that the interior life of feminist Catholics is the "place" where the fierce inner battle over ecclesiastical apartheid is being lived in all its agonizing intensity. The church is certainly involved in an institutional power struggle that is theological and political. But, as with every authentic liberation struggle, at its heart lies a spiritual struggle. In every such struggle the victims must find a way between the Scylla of death-dealing oppression by the power structure they are fighting and the Charybdis of soul-destroying hatred that would make political victory meaningless. Community support is essential in this struggle, but ultimately individuals must face, live through, and emerge from the ultimate threat to their selfhood that the struggle constitutes. Engaging this inner struggle, finding within themselves the truth-power that will make genuine conversion possible, is a major contribution of feminist Catholics whose spirituality has been subsumed into this paschal experience of death in hope of new life.

However, in the passage through the dark night of external oppression and inner desolation it is crucial that the imagination be enlivened with new possibilities. The exiles must have hope, and they cannot sing the songs of Sion in the Babylon of ecclesiastical violence. What Catholic feminists, especially those who are active in Womenchurch, are contributing to the spirituality of women who are both Catholic and feminist is a whole new repertoire of songs, new liturgical forms for the imagination, a proleptic image of a new church. These women have bravely moved ahead and begun to live what they believe, not waiting for permission or until the rest of the church is ready to move. And their living is an assurance that there is reality in the hope of those who live the exile. If exile is the primary self-image for feminist Catholics, exodus is the primary self-image for Catholic feminists.

In fact, there is much mutually empowering interchange between the two groups. While feminist Catholics may sometimes fear that their Womenchurch sisters have "thrown out the baby with the bath" and set sail for a non-existent promised land and Catholic feminists may sometimes deplore what looks like fearful conservatism in their still "churched" sisters, the two groups are increasingly respectful of each other. Not only is internecine struggle among feminists damaging to the movement; it is contrary to the very inclusiveness and connectedness that feminists want to promote and it plays directly into the patriarchal agenda of separating women from women. There is more than one kind of suffering, more than one kind of fear, and more than one kind of courage. The gifts of all must meet the weaknesses of each as the struggle continues.

In regard to the institutional church all women who are both Catholic and feminist desire passionately the conversion of the institution from the sin of sexism and know that this requires a full and final repudiation of patriarchy. Feminist Catholics are struggling to find within the tradition the resources for bringing about this massive transformation. The work of feminist Catholic theologians, ministers, and parents toward this end is carried on in the firm hope that one can use the master's tools to dismantle the master's house and that from the debris of the house of ecclesiastical patriarchy we will be able to construct the home of equal discipleship within which the reign of God can be realized.

By contrast, Catholic feminists tend, if not to give up completely on the institution, to regard it as not worth their life's blood. For them the best way to bring about a new church is to start being that church now. If the real life energy of the church is diverted into the swelling torrent of feminist spirituality, the patriarchal institution will soon be a dried up river bed, an arid trace of a lifeform that refused to change and so remains as a more or less interesting crack in the surface of history. Like other lifeforms that could not change, the patriarchal church will become an interesting historical fossil while the real church moves into the future as a discipleship of equals.

Again, the two approaches are not so much contradictory as complementary. The common aim is a new religious dwelling for the disciples of Jesus. Whether one rebuilds on the ancestral site or buys new land in a distant location is a prudential decision. In either case, a pre-condition of the new construction is that the old hovel of patriarchy must come down because it is unfit for human habitation. What the two groups of feminists in the church have in common is their diagnosis of the problem and their commitment to solving it. While feminist Catholics bring pressure to bear for transformation from within, Catholic feminists are serving notice that if the transformation is not undertaken in earnest, and soon, increasing numbers of believers will look elsewhere for spiritual nourishment.

2. Spirituality as the Place of Crisis for Women Catholics Who Are Feminists

The second conclusion I would draw from the foregoing reflections on the spirituality of women Catholics who are feminists is that spirituality, the lived experience of the faith, is the place of crisis for women whose consciousness is raised as well as for the church as institution.

What began for most women as a problem with the institution has become in recent years a problem of faith. When the first Women's Ordination Conference met in Detroit in 1975 the women who attended were focused on the transformation of the power arrangements in the institutional church specifically through the admission of women to orders. By the time the second Women's Ordination Conference met in Baltimore three years later, the women who attended were already aware that the "add women and stir" recipe for church reform was totally inadequate. Since 1978 women have come to realize that, in reality, we are not talking about how to organize the institution. We are talking about whether the God of Judaeo-Christian revelation is the true God or just men-writ-large to legitimate their domination; whether Jesus, an historical male, is or can be messiah and savior for those who are not male; whether what the church has called sacraments are really encounters with Christ or tools of male ritual abuse of women; whether what we have called church is a community of salvation or simply a male power structure. In other words, because the issue has moved from the realm of politics to the realm of spirituality, the stakes are now very high.

IV. Conclusion

At no time in its history, except perhaps at the time of the Protestant reformation, has the church faced a crisis of such proportions. However, the Protestant reformation involved a relatively small segment of the church in the tiny theater of western Europe. Feminism involves over half the church in every location in the world. All of the mothers of future Catholics are women and, despite the exclusion of women from orders, by far the majority of the church's professional ministers are women. While not all Catholic women are feminists, time and historical process is on the side of rising liberationist consciousness, not on the side of oppressive ideology. The church as institution cannot survive the final disillusionment of women although women, as church, can probably survive the demise of the patriarchal institution. The conclusion is that because the issue is in the arena of

spirituality it must be taken with utter seriousness. If anything is to be learned from the Protestant reformation it is
that when reform is urgent it may be deferred but it cannot
finally be avoided and the price of deferral can be disas-
trously high.

However, precisely because the feminist issue within
the church has resituated itself in the realm of spirituality,
there is some reason to hope that the institutional church
may be able to meet this monumental challenge to grow from
a male power structure imprisoning the word of God into a
fitting locus for the epiphany of the reign of God in this
world. Women who are feminists and Catholics bring to the
church not only a powerful critique and the very real possibility of massive withdrawal but enormous resources for transformation. They bring an image of a renewed church that is
derived from the gospels rather than from imperial Rome, the
feudal middle ages, and the divine right monarchies of the
sixteenth and seventeenth centuries. They also bring a spiritual strength tempered in intense suffering and a loyalty that
has survived twenty centuries of exclusion and oppression.
To this vision of faith and this strength of hope they add a
love of Christ, of the church itself, and of the world that has
fueled a burning commitment to ministry since the earliest
days of the church's history and which is still unquenched
despite what raised consciousness has enabled them to see.

The feminism of Catholic women is both the church's
ultimate and most serious challenge and its best hope for a
future worthy of its gospel roots. When the male disciples of
Jesus returned from the town of Samaria where they had
gone to buy lunch they found Jesus in deep theological conversation with a woman. We are told that they were shocked
and could not imagine what Jesus wanted from a woman or
why he would bother to talk to her. But they knew better than
to challenge Jesus' designs whose horizons were obviously

well beyond their culture-bound ken. So the woman, like other apostles who left boats and nets and father and tax stall to follow Jesus and announce the good news, left her water jar and went off to announce Jesus and to present her fellow townspeople with the only question that really matters: "Can this be the Christ?" Women today are asking this same question of the institutional church. Can you recognize in us, in our persons and in our experience, the image of Christ, and will you choose to act accordingly?

Notes

1. Feminism: Women's Fad or Humanity's Future?

1. For documentation of the extraordinary development of the feminist movement during the 1970s and 1980s see Maria Riley, *Transforming Feminism* (Kansas City: Sheed and Ward, 1989) 28–40.

2. An English translation of *Pacem in Terris* is available in Claudia Carlen, *The Papal Encyclicals 1958–1981* (Salem, NH: McGrath, 1981) 107–129. Reference is to paragraph 41.

3. See Karen Offen, "Defining Feminism—A Comparative Historical Approach," *Signs* 14 (August 1988) 129–132, for the history of the development of the terminology of feminism and distinction between historical women's movements and feminism.

4. See Margaret Galiardi, "Bonding, The Critical Praxis of Feminism," *The Way* 26 (1986) 138. Rosalind Delmar, "What Is Feminism?" in Juliet Mitchell and Ann Oakley, eds., *What IS Feminism?* (Oxford: Basil Blackwell, 1986) 11–13, makes the same point, namely that feminist consciousness is essential to genuine feminist commitment.

5. See Offen, "Defining Feminism," 129, on the problem of defining feminists. See also Judith Stacey, "Are Feminists Afraid to Leave Home? The Challenge of Conservative Pro-family Feminism," in Mitchell and Oakley, eds., *What IS Feminism?* 219–248, on the interesting contemporary phenomenon of backlash among second wave feminist leaders who seem to be retreating from the feminist agenda because of the losses they have suffered within the movement.

6. See Delmar, "What Is Feminism?" in Mitchell and Oakley, eds., *What IS Feminism?* 14–29, on the difference between the emancipation movement and the contemporary women's liberation movement.

7. For a brief history of the ERA which was introduced into Congress in 1923 and is currently dormant, see Riley, *Transforming Feminism,* 31–32.

8. Nancy F. Cott analyzes this seeming anomaly well in "Feminist Theory and Feminist Movements: The Past Before Us," in Juliet Mitchell and Ann Oakley, eds., *What IS Feminism?* 49–62.

9. Various authors assign different dates to the beginning of the "second wave" but all agree that it arose in the 1960s. Juliet Mitchell, "Reflections on Twenty Years of Feminism," in Juliet Mitchell and Ann Oakley, eds. *What IS Feminism?* 34, situates the beginning in 1963 with the publication of Betty Friedan's *The Feminine Mystique.* Riley, *Transforming Feminism,* 25, says that the contemporary women's liberation movement was born in 1967 in Chicago when Jo Freeman and Shulamith Firestone, organizers of the Women's Caucus at the National Conference for New Politics, convened a meeting of women in protest over the ignoring of the women's resolution which they had attempted to introduce at the conference. Sally Purvis, in "Christian Feminist Spirituality," *Christian Spirituality: Post-Reformation and Modern,* Louis Dupré and Don C. Saliers, eds. [*World Spirituality: an Encyclopedic History of the Religious Quest*] vol. 18 (New York: Crossroad, 1989) 500–519, situates the beginning of contemporary Christian feminism in 1968 with the publication of Mary Daly's *The Church and the Second Sex* (San Francisco: Harper and Row, 1968).

10. See Cott, "Feminist Theory and Feminist Movements," 49–62, for discussion of this crucial point.

11. Cott, ibid., explains this dilemma very well. For an excellent personal description as well as analytical exploration of this dilemma, see Ann Snitow, "Pages From a Gender Diary: Basic Divisions in Feminism," *Dissent* 36 (1989) 205–224.

12. Offen, "Defining Feminism," 128, explains well the European feminist preference for women's rights and why the Anglo-

American insistence on individual rights is not generally shared by the continental feminists.

13. Ibid. 123.

14. Offen, ibid., 135–136, argues that the main difference between European feminism and Anglo-American feminism is that the former emphasizes the relational and the latter the individual approach to women's rights.

15. An English translation of John Paul II's *Mulieres Dignitatem* (On the Dignity and Vocation of Women) can be found in *Origins* 18 (October 6, 1988) 261–283.

16. Offen, "Defining Feminism," 119–157, develops this contrast between the characteristically relational approach of European feminists and the characteristically individualist approach of English and American feminists and argues for the equal legitimacy of the European form. She correctly insists that any realistic definition of feminism must take both types into account.

17. See Riley, *Transforming Feminism*, 31–32, for content of the ERA and the specific objections to it which succeeded in preventing its ratification in 1982. See Cott, "Feminist Theory and Feminist Movements: The Past Before Us," 49–62, for a good analysis of the fears of women that the ERA would remove the basis for claiming as a right respect for women's specific needs.

18. Some "base line" definitions of feminism, each of which emphasizes one or more of the elements in the definition I have proposed, have been offered by the following theorists: Delmar, "What Is Feminism?" 8; Mary E. Hunt, "Sharing Feminism: Empowerment or Imperialism?" *Journal of Women and Religion* 1 (Fall 1981) 35; Riley, *Transforming Feminism*, xiv, note 2.

19. Delmar, "What Is Feminism?" 11–16, argues that feminists are ideologically self-conscious and that feminism is at the center rather than at the periphery of their commitment. Jeffrey C. Eaton, "Simone Weil and Feminist Spirituality," *Journal of the American Academy of Religion* 54 (Winter 1986) 692, also insists on self-consciousness as a characteristic of a feminist. Shelley Finson, "Feminist Spirituality Within the Framework of Feminist Consciousness," *Studies in Religion* 16 (1987) 65–66, by emphasizing

the role of feminist consciousness in feminist commitment, makes the same point. By contrast, Mary E. Giles, *The Feminist Mystic and Other Essays on Women and Spirituality* (New York: Crossroad, 1982) 30, equates self-affirmation as a woman, for example as it was exemplified in Teresa of Avila and Catherine of Siena, with feminism. K. Offen, "Defining Feminism," 129–132, correctly in my opinion, regards such a position as both anachronistic and confusing.

20. Finson, "Feminist Spirituality Within the Framework of Feminist Consciousness," 65–66.

21. Ibid. 67–68.

22. Ibid. 67–68.

23. I. Carter Heyward, "Is a Self-Respecting Christian Woman an Oxymoron: Reflections on a Feminist Spirituality for Justice?" *Religion and Intellectual Life* 3 (Winter 1986) 46, says that religious feminists are prone to fall into the trap of trying to pursue personal transformation apart from political involvement but that this connot be effective. Judith Plaskow and Carol P. Christ, eds., *Weaving the Visions: New Patterns in Feminist Spirituality* (San Francisco: Harper and Row, 1989) 11, make the same point.

24. "We can transform ourselves only by simultaneously struggling to transform the social relations that define us: self-changing and changed social institutions are simply two aspects of the same process." Cited by Riley, *Transforming Feminism,* 45, from Nancy Hartsock, "Fundamental Feminism: Process and Perspective," *Building Feminist Theory* (New York: Longman, 1981) 36.

25. Offen, in "Defining Feminism," 129–132, says that the common thread running through the writings of all those who have been called feminists back through history is the "impetus to critique and improve the disadvantaged status of women relative to men within a particular cultural situation" (132). She correctly notes, however, that it is anachronistic to refer to all who have had such an agenda as "feminists," a term which goes back only to the late nineteenth century. I would add that such usage is not only linguistically anachronistic and therefore confusing but that there is a substantive difference between realizing that women are disadvantaged in relation to men and analyzing the systemic nature and

cause of that disadvantage. Contemporary feminism is distinguished from earlier women's movements by its analysis of patriarchy.

26. Riley, *Transforming Feminism,* 46. For a more extensive treatment of the major traditions in contemporary feminism, see Josephine Donovan, *Feminist Theory: The Intellectual Traditions of American Feminism* (New York: Frederick Ungar Publishing Co., 1985). This volume devotes a chapter to each of the following feminist traditions: enlightenment liberal, cultural, Marxist, Freudian, existentialist, and radical.

27. See Stacey, "Are Feminists Afraid to Leave Home? The Challenge of Conservative Pro-family Feminism," 219–248.

28. Riley, *Transforming Feminism,* 64.

29. Ibid. 56–63.

30. See the extraordinarily powerful response of Audre Lorde, "Sexism: An American Disease in Blackface," *Sister Outsider: Essays and Speeches* (Trumansburg, NY: Crossing Press, 1984) 60–65, to an article by Robert Staples, a black sociologist, entitled "The Myth of Black Macho: A Response to Angry Black Feminists," in *The Black Scholar* 10 (March–April, 1979; May–June, 1989) 24–33; 63–67. Staples tried to trivialize the black feminist agenda in relation to the racist issue, and Lorde provides a powerful rebuttal in defense of black feminism. She says, "The results of woman-hating in the Black community are tragedies which diminish all Black people. These acts must be seen in the context of a systematic devaluation of Black women within this society. It is within this context that we become approved and acceptable targets for Black male rage, so acceptable that even a Black male social scientist condones and excuses this depersonalizing abuse.

"This abuse is no longer acceptable to Black women in the name of solidarity, nor of Black liberation. Any dialogue between Black women and Black men must begin there, no matter where it ends" (65).

31. Gerda Lerner, *The Creation of Patriarchy* (New York: Oxford University Press, 1986) 123–130.

32. Nancy J. Chodorow, *The Reproduction of Mothering: Psychoanalysis and the Sociology of Gender* (Berkeley: University of California Press, 1988).

33. Nancy J. Chodorow, *Feminism and Psychoanalytic Theory* (New Haven/London: Yale University Press, 1989) 2–5.

34. Elizabeth Dodson Gray, *Patriarchy as a Conceptual Trap* (Wellesley, MA: Roundtable Press, 1982) 28–29, argues that while men, especially before they became aware that there was a connection between sex and procreation and therefore that the male played a role in reproduction, constructed religions in which female fertility was worshiped, this does not mean that women controlled the myths and symbol systems of these societies.

35. For a more extended analysis of patriarchy as a social structure and its effects on all social organization, see W.A. Visser't Hooft, *The Fatherhood of God in an Age of Emancipation* (Geneva: World Council of Churches, 1982), esp. chapters one to three.

36. Church officials warning against "radical feminism" use the term without much precision. In general they seem to regard as "radical" any feminism which calls into question official church teaching, policy, or practice on the basis of gender analysis. See, e.g., the address, "The Bishop as Teacher of the Faith," by John O'Connor, Cardinal Archbishop of New York, delivered in Rome, March 8, 1989, at the meeting of the pope with the U.S. bishops and carried in *Origins* 18 (March 23, 1989) 283, 285, or John Paul II's letter to the U.S. bishops, "Religious Life in the United States," *Origins* 18 (April 13, 1989) 748.

The U.S. bishops gave evidence of a much more developed understanding of the potential of the feminist analysis of patriarchy to call into question the hierarchical structure of the church in the first draft of "Partners in the Mystery of Redemption: A Pastoral Response to Women's Concerns for Church and Society," *Origins* 17 (April 21, 1988) 787, n. 146. The bishops condemn sexism but refuse to accept a definition of patriarchy as an essentially oppressive structure because "the term *patriarch* has a revered meaning in the hierarchial [sic] titles of the Eastern and Western churches."

Finally, some church officials seem to understand radical as synonymous with fanatical, an equation that has no foundation and reflects official fright rather than reasonable analysis.

37. See Riley, *Transforming Feminism,* 112.

38. For a good collection of essays on the feminist challenge to

the academy, especially in the humanities, see *The New Feminist Criticism: Essays on Women, Literature, and Theory,* ed. Elaine Showalter (New York: Pantheon, 1985). Anne Carr, "The Scholarship of Gender: Women's Studies and Religious Studies," *Transforming Grace: Christian Tradition and Women's Experience* (San Francisco: Harper and Row, 1988) 63-94, explains the effect of the feminist challenge in the area of theology.

39. See reference in n. 9 above.

40. Mary Daly, "The Women's Movement: An Exodus Community," *Religious Education* 67 (September/October 1972) 270-271.

41. In the following paragraphs I am describing the development of feminist consciousness in Catholicism in logical/psychological/theological sequence rather than in strictly chronological sequence.

42. Heyward poses the question in the title of her article, "Is a Self-Respecting Christian Woman an Oxymoron: Reflections on a Feminist Spirituality for Justice," 45-62.

43. Rosemary R. Ruether, in "Feminism and Religious Faith: Renewal or New Creation?" *Religion and Intellectual Life* 3 (Winter 1986) 7-20, outlines the agenda of religious feminism in the form of five questions:

1) How can the elements of the religion be reinterpreted from a female perspective so that they help to make women subjects of their own history?

2) Can religion and spirituality function to enhance the liberationist transformation of history rather than the sacralization of male domination?

3) How can stories and symbols drawn from religious traditions be translated from their androcentric form into one defined by and for women?

4) Should we continue merely to translate from androcentric traditions or do we need to go beyond them and create new stories, new symbols, etc.?

5) Should women remain divided from each other and immured in androcentric traditions or should women unite across religious boundaries in some synthesis of the perspectives traditionally set against each other?

44. Elisabeth Schüssler Fiorenza, in her groundbreaking work, *In Memory of Her: A Feminist Theological Reconstruction of Christian Origins* (New York: Crossroad, 1983), coined this expression which has been taken up as a shorthand formula to describe the alternative feminist vision of Christianity as it derives from the New Testament.

45. Riley, in *Transforming Feminism*, xiii, summarized the Catholic feminist agenda as follows: "For Catholic feminists who choose to remain within the faith tradition, the transformation of the church beyond patriarchy is the enduring agenda. Most of our writings and strategies have been aimed at revealing and transforming the patriarchy of the church as it takes shape in its all-male hierarchy, in its God-language and imagery, its sacramental life, its anthropology, its articulation of a male-defined theological, scriptural, and moral magisterial [sic], and its subtle but all-pervasive misogyny."

46. Two important Catholic contributions to this systematic theological project are Carr, *Transforming Grace,* and Rosemary R. Ruether, *Sexism and God-Talk: Toward a Feminist Theology* (Boston: Beacon, 1983).

47. For a discussion of the challenge being raised by women of color, third world, and lesbian women to the white, middle class, first world feminist perspective, see Purvis, "Christian Feminist Spirituality."

2. Scripture: Tool of Patriarchy or Resource for Transformation?

1. An English translation of *Dei Verbum* is available in *Vatican Council II: The Conciliar Documents,* vol. I, ed. Austin P. Flannery (Grand Rapids, MI: Eerdmans, 1984) 750–765.

2. For a brief, clear presentation of the meaning of fundamentalism in relation to the Bible, see Dianne Bergant, "Fundamentalists and the Bible," *New Theology Review* 1 (May 1988) 35–50. This entire issue is devoted to various aspects of fundamentalism in both Protestantism and Catholicism.

3. See Sallie McFague, *Metaphorical Theology: Models of God in Religious Language* (Philadelphia: Fortress, 1982) 54–66, for a succinct treatment of problems with both fundamentalism and extreme liberalism in relation to scripture.

4. Cf. *Dei Verbum*, VI, 21.

5. Cf. McFague, *Metaphorical Theology*, 31–42, on which the following treatment of metaphor depends heavily.

6. Cf. Paul Ricoeur, *Interpretation Theory: Discourse and the Surplus of Meaning* (Fort Worth, TX: Texas Christian University Press, 1976) 64.

7. McFague, *Metaphorical Theology*, 108–117.

8. See, e.g., Rita J. Burns, *Exodus, Leviticus, Numbers, with Excursuses on Feasts/Ritual and Typology* [Old Testament Message, vol. 3] (Wilmington, DE: Michael Glazier, 1983) 29–36, on the decisive role played by the Hebrew midwives and the mother and sister of Moses in the salvation of the Hebrews from extermination in Egypt.

9. See Elisabeth Schüssler Fiorenza, *In Memory of Her: A Feminist Theological Reconstruction of Christian Origins* (New York: Crossroad, 1983) esp. 118–159.

10. For examples of two different approaches to such texts in the Old Testament, see Phyllis Trible, *Texts of Terror* (Philadelphia: Fortress, 1984) 37–92, and T. Drorah Setel, "Prophets and Pornography: Female Sexual Imagery in Hosea," *Feminist Interpretation of the Bible,* ed. Letty M. Russell (Philadelphia: Westminster, 1985) 86–95.

11. Winsome Munro, in "Women, Text and Canon: The Strange Case of 1 Corinthians 14:33–35," *Biblical Theology Bulletin* 18 (January 1988) 26–31, summarizes the current state of research on such problematic passages in the Pauline and pastoral literature as well as proposing a canonical criticism approach to dealing with them.

12. Ricoeur, *Interpretation Theory*, 78–79, discusses the logic of validation theoretically. Mary Ann Tolbert in *Perspectives on the Parables: An Approach to Multiple Interpretations* (Philadelphia: Fortress, 1979) 111–116, demonstrates the use of criteria in the evaluation of two different interpretations of the parable of the prodigal son.

13. Hans-Georg Gadamer, *Truth and Method* (New York: Seabury, 1975) 289–305.

14. Linnell E. Cady, "Hermeneutics and Traditions: The Role of the Past in Jurisprudence and Theology," *Harvard Theological Review* 79 (October 1986) 439–463.

15. Ricoeur, *Interpretation Theory,* 25–44.

16. Plato in "The Seventh Letter" and in the "Phaedrus" (both available in *The Collected Dialogues of Plato including the Letters,* eds. E. Hamilton and H. Cairns [Princeton, N.J., University Press, 1961]), castigated writing because he regarded the text as being at least three removes from the Forms which it tries to represent. The text, he maintained, cannot dialogue with the reader, and dialogue is the means for coming to true knowledge.

17. Paul Ricoeur, "The Hermeneutical Function of Distanciation," *Hermeneutics and the Human Sciences,* ed. J.B. Thompson (Cambridge: University Press, 1981) 139.

18. The subtitle of Ricoeur's *Interpretation Theory* is *Discourse and the Surplus of Meaning.* He treats the surplus of meaning throughout the work but esp. on pp. 54–57 on "The Semantic Moment of a Symbol."

19. See Gadamer, *Truth and Method,* 253–258, on the notion of "the classical."

20. Ricoeur, "The Hermeneutical Function of Distanciation," 140–142.

21. Interestingly enough, *Dei Verbum* affirms this corporate character of biblical interpretation when it says that growth in insight into the realities and words of the Christian tradition (including scripture) "comes about in various ways. It comes through the contemplation and study of believers who ponder these things in their hearts . . . from the intimate sense of spiritual realities which they experience" (II, 8) while insisting that "the task of giving an authentic interpretation of the Word of God, whether in its written form or in the form of Tradition, has been entrusted to the living teaching office of the Church alone" (II, 10). This is only one of the unresolved tensions in this conciliar document.

22. Cf. Ricoeur, "The Hermeneutical Function of Distanciation," 139.

23. On the essential complementarity of hermeneutics and dialectics see the excellent essay by Matthew Lamb, "The Dialectics of Theory and Praxis Within Paradigm Analysis," in *Paradigm Change in Theology: A Symposium for the Future,* eds. Hans Küng and David Tracy, tr. Margaret Köhl (New York: Crossroad, 1989) 63–109.

24. For a clear and succinct explanation of the use of the prophetic-liberating tradition as a norm by which to criticize the Bible's patriarchal content, see Rosemary Radford Ruether, *Sexism and God-Talk: Toward a Feminist Theology* (Boston: Beacon, 1983) 20–33.

25. See Gadamer, *Truth and Method,* 325–341, on the dialogue as hermeneutical model.

26. See Roland E. Murphy, "Canticle of Canticles," *The New Jerome Biblical Commentary,* ed. Raymond E. Brown, Joseph A. Fitzmyer, Roland E. Murphy (Englewood Cliffs, NJ: Prentice-Hall, 1990) 463.

27. Phyllis Trible, *God and the Rhetoric of Sexuality* (Philadelphia; Fortress, 1978) 144–165.

3. Feminist Spirituality: Christian Alternative or Alternative to Christianity?

1. See Sandra M. Schneiders, "Theology and Spirituality: Strangers, Rivals, or Partners?" *Horizons* 13 (Fall 1986) 257–260.

2. Schneiders, "Theology and Spirituality," 266.

3. Sandra M. Schneiders, "Spirituality in the Academy," *Theological Studies* 50 (December 1989) 684.

4. An English translation of *Inter Insignores* is available as *Declaration on the Admission of Women to the Ministerial Priesthood* (Washington, D.C.: United States Catholic Conference, 1976). See pp. 11–15. See also Sandra M. Schneiders, *Women and the Word* (New York: Paulist Press, 1986) 3–5, on the maleness of Jesus.

5. Catherina Halkes, "Feminism and Spirituality," tr. Joan van der Sman, *Spirituality Today* 40 (1988) 220.

6. Carol P. Christ and Judith Plaskow, eds. *Womanspirit Rising:*

A Feminist Reader in Religion (San Francisco: Harper and Row, 1979).

7. Judith Plaskow and Carol P. Christ, eds., *Weaving the Visions: New Patterns in Feminist Spirituality* (San Francisco: Harper and Row, 1989).

8. Halkes, "Feminism and Spirituality," 220.

9. For a readable but very informative account of the origin of western religion as the religion of the Great Goddess and the gradual triumph of the male warrior God of the Indo-European and Hebrew peoples, see Joseph Campbell with Bill Moyers, *The Power of Myth,* ed. Betty Sue Flowers (New York: Doubleday, 1988) 164–183. For a scholarly discussion of the original supremacy of the Goddess, her eventual replacement by the male God, and the relationship of this trnsformation of mythology to the actual social condition of women, see Gerda Lerner, *The Creation of Patriarchy* (New York: Oxford University Press, 1988) 141-160.

10. Carol P. Christ has been a primary figure in the theoretical development of feminist spirituality both through her literary analyses of women's literature of transformation and through her work on the function of "the goddess" in women's psychological development through the appropriation of inner divine power and outward political power. For examples of her work in these areas, see her essays, "Margaret Atwood: The Surfacing of Women's Spiritual Quest and Vision," *Signs* 2 (Winter 1976) 316-330; "Why Women Need the Goddess: Phenomenological, Psychological, and Political Reflections," in *Womanspirit Rising: A Feminist Reader in Religion,* 273–287.

11. See, for example, the explanations of this fundamental character and agenda of feminist spirituality by Shelley Finson, "Feminist Spirituality Within the Framework of Feminist Consciousness," *Studies in Religion* 16 (1987) 65–77; Patricia Schechter, "Feminist Spirituality and Radical Political Commitment," *Journal of Women and Religion* 4:1 (Spring 1981) 57; Sally B. Purvis, "Christian Feminist Spirituality," *Christian Spirituality: Post-Reformation and Modern,* Louis Dupré and Don E. Saliers, eds. [*World Spirituality: An Encyclopedic History of the Religious Quest*] vol. 18 (New York: Crossroad, 1989) 500–519.

12. See Lerner, *The Creation of Patriarchy,* for a comprehensive treatment.

13. Lerner, *The Creation of Patriarchy,* 36, refers to the hypothesis of an original matriarchy as the creation of a compensatory myth for which there is no compelling evidence. Other feminist scholars who reject the hypothesis of an original matriarchy are the following: Elizabeth Dodson Gray, *Patriarchy as a Conceptual Trap* (Wellesley, MA: Roundtable Press, 1982) 28–29; Halkes, "Feminism and Spirituality," 221; Rosemary R. Ruether, "Feminism and Religious Faith: Renewal or New Creation?" *Religion and Intellectual Life* 3 (Winter 1986) 8; Merlin Stone, "When God Was a Woman," in *Womanspirit Rising: A Feminist Reader in Religion,* 126–130; Deborah Streeter, "The Goddess: Power and Paradox," *Journal of Women and Religion* 1 (Fall, 1981) 13–14.

14. Lerner, *The Creation of Patriarchy,* 145.

15. Ruether, in "Feminism and Religious Faith: Renewal or New Creation?" 9, explains this process, and its continuation in Christianity, as follows: ". . . the more one studies different religious traditions and their early roots, the more one is tempted to suggest that religion itself is essentially a male creation. The male, marginalized from direct participation in the great mysteries of gestation and birth, asserted his superior physical strength to monopolize leisure and culture and did so by creating ritual expressions that duplicated female gestating and birthing roles, but in such a way as to transfer the power of these primary mysteries to himself. This would perhaps explain why mother-goddess figures predominate in early religion, but do not function to give women power. This ritual sublimation of female functions, as transfer of spiritual power over life to males, is continued in Christianity. The central mysteries of Baptism and the Eucharist duplicate female roles in gestation, birth and nourishment, but give the power over the spiritualized expression of these functions to males, and only males who eschew sex and reproduction."

16. Gray, *Patriarchy as a Conceptual Trap,* 26. (This citation is in italics in the original text.)

17. For an accessible but well-developed treatment of Wisdom as a feminine personification of God in the Judaeo-Christian tradi-

tion, see Susan Cady, Marian Ronan, and Hal Taussig, *Sophia: The Future of Feminist Spirituality* (San Francisco: Harper and Row, 1986). Elizabeth Johnson, in "Jesus, Wisdom of God: A Biblical Basis for a Non-Androcentric Christology," *Ephemerides Theologicae Lovanienses,* LX 1:4 (December 1985) 261–294, suggests the theological potential of this biblical tradition for dealing with contemporary problems in christology.

18. Matthew L. Lamb, "The Dialectics of Theory and Praxis Within Paradigm Analysis," in *Paradigm Change in Theology: A Symposium for the Future,* Hans Küng and David Tracy, eds., Margaret Kohl, tr. (New York: Crossroad, 1989) 96.

19. Some feminist spirituality involves a lyrical celebration of the bodily as sacred. See, e.g., Starhawk (Miriam Simos), "Witchcraft and Women's Culture," Christ and Plaskow, eds., *Womanspirit Rising,* 263. See also Elisabeth Schüssler Fiorenza, "Feminist Spirituality, Christian Identity, and Catholic Vision," Christ and Plaskow, eds., *Womanspirit Rising,* 127–138, for the connection between goddess spirituality, which we will take up below, and the reclaiming of the bodily power to give life in the image of divinity.

20. Plaskow and Christ, eds., "Introduction," *Weaving the Visions,* 6–11.

21. I have attempted to distinguish between divinity presented in feminine form and particular feminine personifications of divinity by referring to the former as "Goddess" (without the article and capitalized, as we use the term God) and to the latter as "the goddess" or "a goddess" (with article and in lower case, as we would speak of the gods).

22. In answer to the question of whether Goddess is simply "female power writ large" or a real entity, Carol Christ, in "Why Women Need the Goddess," Christ and Plaskow, eds. *Womanspirit Rising,* 278–279, replies that different women answer that question differently. Some see Goddess as a real divine protectress to whom one can pray. Others see her primarily as symbol of either life-death-rebirth or of the beauty and legitimacy of female power.

23. Miriam Simos, who is a leading practitioner and theorist of witchcraft and who is known by her wicca name of Starhawk, provides an excellent explanation of this ancient religious tradition

and its fate in Christian Europe in "Witchcraft and Women's Culture," in Christ and Plaskow, eds., *Womanspirit Rising,* 259–268.

24. Ibid. 261–262.

25. Ibid. 263.

26. Rosemary Radford Ruether, in "Feminist Theology and Spirituality," in *Christian Feminism: Visions of a New Humanity,* Judith L. Weidman, ed. (San Francisco: Harper and Row, 1984) 11, puts it well: "Feminist theology starts with the affirmation that God, the ground of being and new being, underlies, includes, supports, and promotes female personhood as much as male personhood. Woman is not subordinate or 'included under,' but equivalent as imago dei."

27. An important contribution to this discussion is Christine Downing's *The Goddess: Mythological Images of the Feminine* (New York: Crossroad, 1981).

28. An excellent study on the goddesses as archetypes of the feminine is Jean Shinoda Bolen's *Goddesses in Every Woman: A New Psychology of Women* (San Francisco: Harper and Row, 1984).

29. Cf. Elizabeth Dreyer, "Recovery of the Feminine in Spirituality," *New Catholic World* 227 (1984) 71–72. Purvis, in "Christian Feminist Spirituality," 503–504, calls story-telling the creative moment in Christian feminist spirituality.

30. See, e.g., Christ, "Margaret Atwood," in Christ and Plaskow, eds., *Womanspirit Rising,* 329–330, who insists, in regard to menstruation, pregnancy, and childbirth, that "it seems to me far wiser for women as persons and as critics to name the power which resides in our bodies and our potential closeness to nature positively, and to use this new naming to transform the pervasive cultural and religious devaluation of nature and the body."

Purvis, in "Christian Feminist Spirituality," 504–514, names "embodiment" as one of the major characteristics of feminist spirituality. It involves a rejection of male fear of sexuality and an embracing of the erotic as a source of passion for union in love, for social justice, and for encountering God.

Schüssler Fiorenza, describing the effect of goddess consciousness, says in "Feminist Spirituality, Christian Identity, and Catholic Vision," in Christ and Plaskow, eds., *Womanspirit Rising,* 127–138:

"The Goddess is the giver and nurturer of life, the dispenser of love and happiness. Woman as her image is therefore not 'the other' of the divine. She is not body and carnality in opposition to spirit and soul, not the perpetuator of evil and rebellion. Being a woman, living in sisterhood under the aegis of the Goddess, brings us in touch with the creative, healing, life-giving power at the heart of the world."

31. Cf. Streeter, "The Goddess: Power and Paradox," 9; Riley, *Transforming Feminism,* 97, says, "For radical feminism, the primary root [of war] is men's will to dominate women. From this root come all other forms of domination. The will to dominate appears subtly in the patriarchal social structures and the cultural ideology that supports those structures. It appears overtly in all acts of violence: rape, torture, sexual abuse, incest, pornography, domestic violence, the destruction of the earth. It finds its ultimate expression in war. . . ."

32. Some authors who explicate this connection are the following: Margaret Galiardi, "Bonding, The Critical Praxis of Feminism," *The Way* 26 (1986) 134-44; Patricia Schechter, "Feminist Spirituality and Radical Political Commitment," *Journal of Women and Religion* 4:1 (Spring 1981) 51-60; Rosemary R. Ruether, "Feminism and Religious Faith: Renewal or New Creation?" *Religion and Intellectual Life* 3 (Winter 1986) 7-20; Dermot A. Lane, "Christian Feminism," *Furrow* 36 (November 1985) 663-675; Plaskow and Christ, eds. "Introduction," *Weaving the Visions,* 1-11 and Maria Riley, *Transforming Feminism* (Kansas City: Sheed and Ward, 1989).

33. Purvis, "Christian Feminist Spirituality," 509.

34. I suspect most feminists would not recognize as feminist the approach taken by Mary E. Giles, in *The Feminist Mystic and Other Essays on Women and Spirituality* (New York: Crossroad, 1982) 5. Giles objects to much of contemporary feminism and reveals her own approach, which most feminists would label at least anachronistic, when she says, on p. 30, "Catherine and Teresa were free, joyous, loving and creative, alive in and through their being women. As such they were feminists."

35. One can see this kind of development, for example, in the

work of Joann Wolski Conn who, in her first major work on spirituality, *Women's Spirituality: Resources for Christian Development* (New York: Paulist, 1986) 8–27, was hesitant to use the term "feminist" and preferred to speak of "women's spirituality." However, she has since become quite explicitly feminist in her treatment of spirituality. See e.g., "Discipleship of Equals: Past, Present and Future?" *Horizons* 14 (Fall 1987) 231–261.

36. Carol Christ, in the chapter "A Spirituality for Women," in *Laughter of Aphrodite: Reflections on a Journey to the Goddess* (San Francisco: Harper and Row, 1987) 56–72, describes this process as she experienced it. In her case it led to an abandonment of the Christian tradition in favor of Goddess spirituality.

37. A very good personal account of this type of journey is given by Riley in *Transforming Feminism,* 1–11.

38. See Fran Ferder, "Zeal for Your House Consumes Me: Dealing with Anger As a Woman in the Church," *Women in the Church I,* ed. Madonna Kolbenschlag (Washington, D.C.: Pastoral Press, 1987) 95–113 for a discussion of the psychological as well as spiritual dimensions of this experience.

39. In Joann Wolski Conn, ed., *Women's Spirituality: Resources for Christian Development* (New York: Paulist Press, 1986) 287–311.

40. Carolyn Osiek, *Beyond Anger: On Being a Feminist in the Church* (New York: Paulist, 1986).

41. Sandra M. Schneiders, "Women and Power in the Church: A New Testament Reflection," *Proceedings of the Catholic Theological Society of America* 37 (June 10–13, 1982) 123–128.

42. Sandra M. Schneiders, "The Effects of Women's Experience on Their Spirituality," *Spirituality Today* 35 (Summer 1983) 100–116.

43. See Kathleen Fischer, *Women at the Well: Feminist Perspectives on Spiritual Direction* (New York: Paulist, 1988) 175–194.

44. For a good treatment of the impact of feminist scholarship on the theological academy see Carr, *Transforming Grace,* 63–94.

45. This fact has been recognized by the undertaking by the U.S. bishops of the writing of a pastoral letter on women's concerns. See

National Conference of Catholic Bishops, "Partners in the Mystery of Redemption: A Pastoral Response to Women's Concerns for Church and Society," *Origins* 17 (April 21, 1988) 758–788.

46. See "Women-Church: A Feminist Exodus Community," in Rosemary R. Ruether, *Women-Church: Theology and Practice of Feminist Liturgical Communities* (San Francisco: Harper and Row, 1986) 57–74, for a succinct summary description and analysis of the history and present shape of this movement.

47. Cf. Ruether, "Feminism and Religious Faith: Renewal or New Creation?" 17.

Works Cited

Bolen, Jean Shinoda. *Goddesses in Every Woman: A New Psychology of Women*. San Francisco: Harper and Row, 1984.

Cady, Susan, Marian Ronan and Hal Taussig. *Sophia: The Future of Feminist Spirituality*. San Francisco: Harper and Row, 1986.

Campbell, Joseph with Bill Moyers. *The Power of Myth*. Betty Sue Flowers, ed. New York: Doubleday, 1988.

Carr, Anne E. *Transforming Grace: Christian Tradition and Women's Experience*. San Francisco: Harper and Row, 1988.

Christ, Carol P. "Margaret Atwood: The Surfacing of Women's Spiritual Quest and Vision." *Signs* 2 (Winter 1976) 316–330.

―――. *The Laughter of Aphrodite*. San Francisco: Harper and Row, 1987.

――― and Judith Plaskow, eds. *Womanspirit Rising: A Feminist Reader in Religion*. San Francisco: Harper and Row, 1979.

Conn, Joann Wolski. "Discipleship of Equals: Past, Present and Future?" *Horizons* 14 (Fall 1987) 231–61.

―――. *Women's Spirituality: Resources for Christian Development*. New York: Paulist Press, 1986.

Daly, Mary. *The Church and the Second Sex*. San Francisco: Harper and Row, 1968.

————. "The Women's Movement: An Exodus Community." *Religious Education* 67 (September/October 1972) 265–271.

Donovan, Josephine. *Feminist Theory: The Intellectual Traditions of American Feminism*. New York: Frederick Ungar Publishing Co., 1985.

Downing, Christine. *The Goddess: Mythological Images of the Feminine*. New York: Croassroad, 1981.

Dreyer, Elizabeth. "Recovery of the Feminine in Spirituality." *New Catholic World* 227 (1984) 68–72.

Eaton, Jeffrey C. "Simone Weil and Feminist Spirituality." *Journal of the American Academy of Religion* 54 (Winter 1986) 691–704.

Eigo, F.A., ed. *A Discipleship of Equals: Toward a Christian Feminist Spirituality*. Philadelphia: Villanova University Press, 1988.

Ferder, Fran. "Zeal for Your House Consumes Me: Dealing with Anger as a Woman in the Church." *Women in the Church I*, Madonna Kolbenschlag, ed. Washington, D.C.: Pastoral Press, 1987, 56–72.

Finson, Shelley. "Feminist Spirituality within the Framework of Feminist Consciousness." *Studies in Religion* 16 (1987) 65–77.

Fiorenza, Elisabeth Schüssler. *In Memory of Her: A Feminist Theological Reconstruction of Christian Origins*. New York: Crossroad, 1983.

Fischer, Kathleen. *Women at the Well: Feminist Perspectives on Spiritual Direction*. New York: Paulist Press, 1988.

Galiardi, Margaret. "Bonding, The Critical Praxis of Feminism." *The Way* 26 (1986) 134–144.

Giles, Mary. *The Feminist Mystic and Other Essays on Women and Spirituality.* New York: Crossroad, 1982.

Gray, Elizabeth Dodson. *Patriarchy as a Conceptual Trap.* Wellesley, MA: Roundtable Press, 1982.

Halkes, Catharina. "Feminism and Spirituality." Joan ven der Sman, tr. *Spirituality Today* 40 (1988) 22–36.

Hartsock, Nancy. "Fundamental Feminism: Process and Perspective." *Building Feminist Theory.* New York: Longman, 1981, 3–19.

Heyward, I. Carter. "Is a Self-Respecting Christian Woman an Oxymoron? Reflections on Feminist Spirituality for Justice." *Religion and Intellectual Life* 3 (Winter 1986) 45–62.

Hunt, Mary E. "Sharing Feminism: Empowerment or Imperialism?" *Journal of Women and Religion* 1 (Fall 1981) 33–46.

John Paul II. "Mulieres Dignitatem" (On the Dignity and Vocation of Women). *Origins* 18 (October 6, 1988) 261–283.

———. "Religious Life in the United States." *Origins* 18 (April 13, 1989) 74–75.

Johnson, Elizabeth. "Jesus, the Wisdom of God: A Biblical Basis for a Non-Androcentric Christology." *Ephemerides Theologicae Lovanienses.* LX 1:4 (December 1985) 261–294.

Lamb, Matthew L. "The Dialectics of Theory and Praxis Within Paradigm Analysis." *Paradigm Change in Theology: A Symposium for the Future,* Hans Küng and David Tracy, eds., Margaret Kohl, tr. New York: Crossroad, 1989, 63–109.

Lane, Dermot A. "Christian Feminism." *Furrow* 36 (November 1985) 663–675.

Lerner, Gerda. *The Creation of Patriarchy.* New York: Oxford University Press, 1986.

Lorde, Audre. *Sister Outsider: Essays and Speeches.* Trumansburg, NY: Crossing Press, 1984.

Mitchell, Juliet and Ann Oakley, eds. *What IS Feminism?* Oxford: Basil Blackwell, 1986.

National Conference of Catholic Bishops. "Partners in the Mystery of Redemption: A Pastoral Response to Women's Concerns for the Church and Society." *Origins* 17 (April 21, 1988) 757, 759–788.

O'Connor, John. "The Bishop as Teacher of the Faith." *Origins* 18 (March 23, 1989) 283–284.

Offen, Karen. "Defining Feminism—A Comparative Historical Approach." *Signs* 14 (August 1988) 119–157.

Osiek, Carolyn. *Beyond Anger: On Being a Feminist in the Church.* New York: Paulist Press, 1986.

Plaskow, Judith and Carol P. Christ, eds. *Weaving the Visions: New Patterns in Feminist Spirituality.* San Francisco: Harper and Row, 1989.

Purvis, Sally. "Christian Feminist Spirituality." *Christian Spirituality: Post-Reformation and Modern,* Louis Dupré and Don E. Saliers, eds. [World Spirituality: An Encyclopedic History of the Religious Quest] vol. 18 (New York: Crossroad, 1989) 500–519.

Ruether, Rosemary R. "Feminism and Religious Faith: Renewal or New Creation?" *Religion and Intellectual Life* 3 (Winter 1986) 7–20.

———. *Sexism and God-Talk: Toward a Feminist Theology.* Boston: Beacon Press, 1983.

———. *Women-Church: Theology and Practice of Feminist Liturgical Communities.* San Francisco: Harper and Row, 1986.

Riley, Maria. *Transforming Feminism.* Kansas City: Sheed and Ward, 1989.

Schechter, Patricia. "Feminist Spirituality and Radical Political Commitment." *Journal of Women and Religion* 4:1 (Spring 1981) 51–60.

Schneiders, Sandra M. "Spirituality in the Academy." *Theological Studies* 50 (December 1989) 676–697.

———. "The Effects of Women's Experience on Their Spirituality." *Spirituality Today* 35 (Summer 1983) 100–116.

———. "Theology and Spirituality: Strangers, Rivals, or Partners?" *Horizons* 13 (Fall 1986) 253–274.

———. "Women and Power in the Church: A New Testament Reflection." *Proceedings of the Catholic Theological Society of America.* 37 (June 10–13, 1982) 123–128.

———. *Women and the Word: The Gender of God in the New Testament and the Spirituality of Women.* New York: Paulist Press, 1986.

Snitow, Ann. "Pages from a Gender Diary: Basic Divisions in Feminism," *Dissent* 36 (1989) 205–224.

Staples, Robert. "The Myth of Black Macho: A Response to Angry Black Feminists." *The Black Scholar* 10 (March–April, 1979; May–June, 1979) 24–33; 63–67.

Showalter, Elaine, ed. *The New Feminist Criticism: Essays on Women, Literature and Theory.* New York: Pantheon, 1985.

Streeter, Deborah. "The Goddess: Power and Paradox." *Journal of Women and Religion* 1 (Fall 1981) 5–14.

Visser't Hooft, W. A. *The Fatherhood of God in an Age of Emancipation.* Geneva: World Council of Churches, 1982.

Weidman, Judith, ed. *Christian Feminism: Visions of a New Humanity.* San Francisco: Harper and Row, 1984.